Here and Coming

...as it is in heaven.

by Bill Atwood

George —
With prayers and thanks
for your great support and
partnership in the Gospel
+ Bill

Ekklesia

Ekklesia Society Publications
P.O. Box 118526
Carrollton, TX 75011-8526

For all book orders:
www.ekk.org
or
www.amazon.com

ISBN 978-0-9677635-5-2

Ekklesia Publications
PO Box 118526
Carrollton, TX 75011-8526

The original watercolor for the front cover
was painted by Ann Heckenlaible.

Here and Coming

...as it is in heaven.

Section 1

Chapter One
There Has to be More

That which reveals the Kingdom of God is sometimes found in leather bound theology books, but revelation is just as likely to be found in the circumstances of life. Things happen all around us. Often, we fail to make a connection between temporal events and things eternal. Sometimes by grace, however, the Spirit stirs an insight of understanding about the Scriptures, the Kingdom, or the Lord Himself.

It was late. I had gone over to be with Tim again. He was 27 but looked closer to 40. He was shivering and sweating. His face was etched with a grimace that told the story of the depth of his pain. He always put on a bold face, but pneumocystic pneumonia was destroying him. His immune system was shot. Tim's party-friends and his "partner" had pretty much abandoned him when he got sick. New friends weren't much of a possibility. Not too many people want to strike up a relationship with someone dying of AIDS. The only relief came when I would sit with him, holding him carefully in my arms and rocking him, wiping away the sweat from his face with a cool cloth, trying not to hurt his fragile frame. His body had melted down to the point where he seemed more the size of a child than an adult. I could feel the angular stab of his bones against my side and knew that touching him too roughly would not only be horribly painful but would leave terrible bruises.

There had been other nights like this one--rocking and talking and sitting together. But the previous conversations I'd had with him were relatively superficial. Up to now, we had just been getting to know each other and I was endeavoring to serve him in practical, non-verbal ways.

I was waiting for the "quickening" that comes when the Holy Spirit opens an opportunity to share the Gospel. I wish I could claim some saintly pastoral motivations on my part, but the truth is that it was probably more guilt working in me at first. I was embarrassed at my own lack of concern and care that we evangelicals offer to AIDS patients. As Tim and I spent more time together, however, my heart changed. I found in him a man that was worthy of celebration, notwithstanding the death that would soon claim him.

This night would be different. As I held him, I felt his body tense and become rigid. His pain was getting worse and he was starting to decline. He turned and looked at me intensely. After a long, poignant pause he said, "There is something I want to ask. I know you love me and I know you'll tell me the truth." I waited, then he continued, "Does God hate me?"

I paused for a minute, not so much hesitant as to what I should say, but rather to discern the rhythm of the moment and the right words. The words flowed, "No, Tim, He doesn't hate you. In fact, He loves you deeply and unconditionally—even uproariously. He loves you beyond your imagination. He loves you beyond your capacity to sin."

"But," he said, with a look that revealed he sensed the smell of his death close-by, "I'm dying and it's at my own hand. It is the lifestyle I led that is killing me. Is this God's judgment?"

"No," I replied. "Actions have consequences. We are seeing that now. But the circumstances surrounding your life are different from your relationship with God. The fact that you care what God thinks about you speaks volumes. If you feel separated from Him, you can change that. You can return the love He is offering to you. You can choose to trust Him for forgiveness, acceptance, and new life. You can receive Him and His promises right now."

The more I explained the Gospel to him and what it meant to repent, turn around, and commit to Christ, the more radiant he became. By the end of the conversation it was obvious that Tim was a completely different person—changed, reborn, and made new. We prayed together, hugged, and cried. He continued to develop a voracious appetite for the things of the Lord. He began to ask me questions; he wanted to know everything.

I don't know exactly at what point it is in a conversation like that God actually accomplishes the "borning againing". Evangelistically speaking, it was a wonderful triumph. I think back on that remarkable night with a great deal of satisfaction, but there has always been a troublesome, lingering thought. I told Tim about Jesus, but I *wasn't* Jesus to him. I told him how to inherit eternal life, but I couldn't say, "Rise and walk," with the simplicity, confidence, or effectiveness of the Master.

As wonderful as it was to watch Tim's transformation, and as comforting as it was knowing that he died peacefully, I couldn't deliver the same kind of healing that he could have received from Jesus; I wasn't Jesus and this wasn't Galilee. The parade of people who came to Jesus got ever so much more than Tim got from his conversations with me. It wasn't that I doubted that God *could* heal him or even raise the dead. I had, on occasion, experienced wonderful miracles and seen dramatic healings, but I knew there was more available.

My experience had been that there was a madding randomness to answered prayers and works of wonder. They happened, albeit too infrequently, and there was some small comfort in that. But that power only sparked occasionally. Theologically, I knew it was important that Jesus did not do his miracles, signs, and wonders because He was God, but He did them in His fully human nature by being completely submitted to the will of the Father and unreservedly open to the power of the Holy Spirit. I had the theological sense that more was possible to me, but it remained theory.

I didn't really know exactly what it was I was hungry for, but I had the nagging sense of falling short of the possibilities. What was supposed to be the full-blown river of God bringing wonders was more like a trickle. Somehow I knew God has intended for us to experience more. I am not saying that there were never flashes of inspiration or fantastically wonderful miraculous breakthroughs on occasion, but those paled in comparison to the accounts of Jesus' ministry. Whole towns were impacted; everyone was healed. In a way, the spiritual fireworks we periodically see today only make the situation more frustrating. They show that it is possible for God to work supernaturally. The question is *how* might He work and *when*? Even more exciting, *how much* might He be willing to work?

We are living in a time of many answered prayers. Some are dramatically answered. It is a time of "Signs and Wonders," but it is not the way it is described in the Bible. There is every indication that we should be seeing much more. Instead, we see "Signs," and we then "Wonder." Hardly the fulfillment of Jesus' commission to release His power in order to change the world when He said:

> The works that I do you shall also do and greater works because I go to the Father.[1]

Despite the conviction that Jesus is telling the truth, there is a desire for more. Sadly, we are not there yet. Like many others, I am desperately hungry for "it." I know we are making progress and learning about what needs to happen; but, for now, there are still ways in which it is a hunger that is unfulfilled. Sometimes it seems so close that I can taste it, but that is not enough. There is a deep yearning—a longing to receive everything that the Cross has won,

---

[1] John 14:12

4

share every gift that the Spirit gives, and see God glorified through lives being changed. Along the way, some experiences bring transformation and bring the realities of the Kingdom more into focus. Sometimes there are events that help us take significant steps toward the Kingdom coming on earth.

Heaven Bows Down
Iraq

Before the war in Iraq, while Saddam Hussein was still in power, I was invited to go there to teach transferable concepts on how to establish churches with evangelistic house groups. Even though the environment was widely viewed as "moderate" Islam at the time, traditional church planting was impossible. Rather than being truly moderate, the situation was oppressive and very dangerous. Even though most Iraqis are moderate Muslims, some are militant and violent. Bands of militants would occasionally appear to intimidate people or worse. There was almost total unemployment and virtually no functional economy. Every day, people would go to the village square with possessions that had been bought in better times and barter them for food or fuel. The only people working were either "guns-for-hire" or taxi drivers.

On one of the days when it seemed that clashes between the two rival groups were minimal, we drove from the village of Shaqlawa to Koisenjak. It was a beautiful day with crisp air and an azure sky unblemished with even a single cloud. As we slowed for a tight turn at a bend in the road, a group of "peshmerga" (citizen soldiers) burst from a clump of trees with the ubiquitous Russian-made AK-47 Kalashnikov machine guns shouting and violently gesturing for us to stop. In an area with no police, no fire department, no mail delivery, and everyone armed, it was impossible to ignore their demand. As we stopped, the shouting and gesturing intensified. While most of them stood with guns leveled at us, a small group met with one of our interpreters. Over the next few minutes we learned that they were incensed that an RPG (rocket propelled grenade) had been stolen from the house of one of the leaders. They explained that the penalty for such a theft was death.

"No problem," I said, "we were many kilometers away in Shaqlawa last night. Lots of people saw us there; we couldn't have stolen the RPG."

"No matter," the interpreter said. Their rudimentary system of strong-arm "justice" only required that the penalty for such a grievous offence was death. It didn't much matter to them who died. Things turned from bad to worse as the shouting increased. Even during a lull when the leaders gathered in a huddle, the tension was palpable. We were still being held under gunpoint when the deliberations broke up and the group came back. With surreal calm and almost indifference, one of them said, "You are sentenced to death by firing squad." We couldn't really understand the language he had spoken but the machine guns being cocked and aimed at us made it clear.

A lot was happening in a very short time. I thought back to our "family meeting" before I left when we told our teenage daughters that my trip was very dangerous and that there was no guarantee I would come back. I thought back to my daughter who said, "Dad, if you don't come back, you have taught us and showed us who Jesus is and how to live. We will be okay. But we are also going to pray that you come home!"

The situation was very bad, but there was also something inviting about it. Despite the horrors of the day it was a compelling place to be. The presence of God was tangible—exciting—even magnetic. I remember turning to the guy right next to me and saying to him

6

with genuine surprise, "This is easier than I thought it would be." And I watched the scene before me unfold almost with detachment and a "peace that passes understanding" as they cocked their weapons.

Just before they were about to fire, our driver ran in front of the guns shouting. I couldn't understand what he was saying, of course, but later found out that he was shouting, "No, no, these are good men, you cannot shoot them!"

There was a surprised pause as he pressed his chest against the barrel of the gun that a nervous 15 year old had aimed directly at me. Now in between the gun and me, I thought he was going to die. He turned over his shoulder and quietly said, "Leave." But I objected to my friends, saying, "If we die I know what will happen to us, but he is a Muslim."

Again he insisted, "It's alright, go."

Something in his calm insistence made it seem reasonable to leave, so we did. We went just over a small hill and waited. In a few minutes he came beaming over the hilltop, all smiles.

"See," he said, "I told you it would be alright!"

We celebrated and hooted, hugging and dancing each other around with unapologetic abandon and unbridled enthusiasm that seemed worthy of King David twirling before the Lord and the Ark of the Covenant.

As we tried to decompress from the ordeal, we were shown a market that was still called the Old Jewish Market. People explained to us that it dated back to 600 BC when the Jews were brought in to Babylonian captivity. God's fingerprints were present throughout the land.

Imagine the depth of joy to receive a message sent in coded imagery that this heroic driver had "made the decision to go swimming" and that now "there were nine heroes in his village" — nine Christians believing and baptized. He laydown his life. It resulted not only in our rescue, but also kindled a fire. Jesus said,

> Greater love has no one than this, than to lay down one's life for his friends.[2]

His actions had kindled a fire that led to my rescue. But that kind of fire keeps building. The powerful memory, however, is not in being rescued; it is of the tangible presence of God, and the sense of standing in the Kingdom, not just near to it.

In general, we do not do well with this tension. It's not just that we've inherited the fallen moral compass of our forefathers; it's worse than that. We are actually hunched over and contorted--a sad distortion of what we were meant to be. From heaven's perspective, the inhabitants of the earth all look bent. We are not left, however, without hope. Occasionally there will be flashes of Kingdom inspiration.

Where we fall short, The Holy One does not look at us with disgust or revulsion; instead, compassion rises in Him. The Heart that defines what love is stands just as eager to see us restored as He was eager to create us from nothing in the first place. From the human perspective, our brokenness looks bad, but the reality of it is even worse. It's not just that we don't do the things that we were intended to do—we can't. We don't see problems and opportunities the way we should. We don't see with the eyes of Jesus. We don't think with the rhythms of the Kingdom and we don't tap into the possibilities of the Kingdom. Jesus makes it clear

---

[2] John 15:13

in John that at first, we can't even see the Kingdom of God because of being "hunched over." After we are born of the Spirit, we may have the capacity to see, but mostly we don't "get it"—we don't really *see* what we are supposed to see.

When we were first created, it was with the purpose that we would have intimate fellowship with the One who created us. We were made in His image and likeness. Of course, that doesn't mean that we looked like Him, it means that we were of the same fiber, purpose, and agenda. He made us so that we could emulate His character and creativity. In his wonderful book, *Created for Influence* Will Ford writes about this:

> All human beings are spiritual beings, whether they choose to acknowledge that fact or not. All of us are made in the image and likeness of God and our spirits long to connect with the unseen world.[3]

He made us to extend dominion across the earth. In the mind of God, the office of priest was created to make offerings to Him. At first, the offerings were not sin offerings—there was no need because sin had not yet invaded. The first offerings were breathtaking, hilarious celebrations of the fruitfulness of the Kingdom. The offering was to lord over the earth, be sub-masters of creation and offer back to the Master the creative, bountiful fruit that was being produced in it. It was not to be an offering of toil, for there was no toil yet. It was more simple than that. We were just to wave our arms in a sweeping gesture and simply say, "This is all for You. The grapes, butterflies, doves, and watermelons. The orchids, quartz crystals, waterfalls and wildebeest all reflect Your creative genius. This is all an expression of Your great power and

---

[3] William L. Ford, III, *Created for Influence,* (Grand Rapids: Chosen Books, 2007). Page 43.

magnificent love. So we cry, 'All things come of You, O Lord, and of Thine own have we given Thee.'"[4] Originally, we didn't have to till the ground, swing a scythe, gather, grind, or bake; and we didn't have to kill and burn or pour out blood. All we had to do was declare the truth of what is, maybe dance a little jig for joy, and smile back at Father as He put our offering on His refrigerator door.

But, we missed the boat. Well, we didn't just miss it, we trashed it. We scuttled the opportunity because the original two people succumbed to the serpent's wiles. Don't get me wrong, their sin was devastating but we really shouldn't feel all that superior to them. First of all, they didn't have much of a chance. A careful reading of the temptation scene in Genesis shows that the Serpent hit them with all of the temptations of all the deadly sins. The fruit he polished and offered seduced them with greed, lust, gluttony, pride, and more. Since they had freedom, they were not *forced* to obey. They were given the choice to do so. Tragically, they failed. But, they were not alone in their rebellion. Each one of us has demonstrated that we are not of any superior stock. Given the same test in our day, we have failed just as certainly and proven that "all have sinned and fallen short of the glory of God."[5]

Our legacy is separation from God, but it is more than that. It is death. It is sickness and so much more. It is bondage, addiction, and despair. It is a distortion of the very purpose for which we were created. Not only do we fail to fulfill our potential, but we are also stunted, and in our bowed down state, are continually looking down. We don't see what we are supposed to see, let alone do what we are supposed to do.

---

[4] 1 Chronicles 29:14
[5] Romans 3:23

But Jesus does not leave us comfortless. He gives us the gift of the Holy Spirit to give us new birth into the Kingdom of God. Much more than just being given a ticket to heaven (though in salvation we certainly get that), we are given a new life. We are given new sight. Jesus said, "If you are not born of the Spirit you cannot even see the Kingdom of God." If we *are* born of the Spirit, there is a *revolution!* Now for the first time, we have at least the possibility of seeing things as they really are. Reality stretches *way* beyond normal sight. It is found in the kind of Kingdom vision that sees past the concrete into the eternal. It sees beyond the situation to eternal implications. It's the kind of vision that understands that a sculpture may more fully reflect the essence of flight than a plane, or that a passage of music may convey pathos better than words alone. It is the kind of sight that can see past tragedy and anguish, and muster the hope not only to go on but to believe in real victory.

> "I would have lost heart, unless I had believed that I would see the goodness of the LORD in the land of the living."[6]

It's not just that there is hope for Heaven; our spirit dares to hope that it is not just *then,* but it is *now* as well.

Knowing that we are fallen and in anguish (even if we don't see it), Jesus shows Himself to be "my glory and the One who lifts up my head."[7] With the encouragement of our chins being lifted and our gaze raised to survey Heaven's priorities and principles, we can move into new Godly possibilities and horizons. We are given something new that is very old. We are offered our original purpose. We are redeemed and restored. We are taken back to the moment before we fell, even before our ancestors fell. We are taken back to the garden and our original marching orders:

---

[6] Psalm 27:13
[7] Psalm 3:3

"Be fruitful and multiply; fill the earth and subdue it; have dominion over the fish of the sea, over the birds of the air, and over every living thing that moves on the earth."[8]

Our creative purpose is renewed. We are not just forgiven and given a visa for eternal life. More than just being dusted off and sent back out like a coach encourages and re-deploys a player who has fallen into the mud, we are forgiven and transfigured. We are offered a baptism of fire of such intensity that it can burn away the shackles that have bound our potential and kept us mere caricatures of what we were intended to be.

In our natural state, born into the world in sin, we are seed beds for disappointment. We are Petri dishes cultivating new moldy ways to have sin tarnish our lives and spreading anguish, pain, and death to those around us. The effects of sin are passed on as surely as a terminal disease that is passed genetically from father to son or mother to daughter. Though we retain the capacity to do some things that are good, all things that we do are tainted by sin. Every arena of human life bears the stain. Sometimes things are so totally out of control that even the sensibilities of the unregenerate are skewed.

Rwanda Genocide

Rwanda, in East Africa, was a place of great promise. It had been pretty successfully evangelized. It was thought of as the most Christianized nation on the planet. More than 90% of the population claimed to be Christian. But these were not necessarily converted or discipled people. It may not be meaningless that they identified their lives with Christ in some way, but their Christian

---

[8] Genesis 1:28

values didn't stop one hundred days of horror when eight hundred thousand people were killed, mostly hacked to death with machetes. The conflict spilled over into neighboring Burundi and another two hundred thousand died, as well.

The depth of the tragedy really hit me when I visited Ntyrama. There, a memorial church stands that was left as it was after five thousand Tutsi and moderate Hutu tribal members were killed by radical Hutus in the span of 100 days. Violence had gripped the country and people fled to the church in Ntyrama for comfort and protection. Thousands came summoned by a traitorous pastor in league with the murderous rebels. There in God's house they were shot, stabbed, hacked to death, and simply left where they fell. When I stood there at the church, it was only about a year after the hundred days of genocidal hell and the bodies were still there. The flesh had decayed away in the African heat, but the bones hadn't moved. In many cases, people's clothes were still intact with grisly scenes of skeletons poking out of shirtsleeves, dresses, and trouser legs.

Only the Gospel of Christ can work to begin to heal such a wound. Not just the superficial platitudes of a religious-club-church, but the real transforming power that could fill people with new life and new Love; the Christ-love that can allow people to forgive and love those who murdered their family. No wound ever had greater need for divine grace. It is only the supernatural power of the Kingdom than can turn hearts to become willing to love murderers into forgiveness and wholeness.

One of the men working in that desperate environment to disciple people in Christ, who is clear about the task, is Bishop John Ruchyahana. He is an Anglican bishop who is sharing the Word of life. He has worked to open orphanages and even his own home and family to share love and meet needs in people's lives. He is a man of modest physical stature, but significant in the Kingdom.

One day we were talking about the struggles in Rwanda and the parallels in the United States as the culture seeks to snuff out real Christian faith and virtue. He knows that awful circumstances, as hideous as they are, can also provide the opportunity for people to rise to the occasion and reflect Christ. I'll never forget John saying to me, "Bill, if you had been born in Africa, you would have been taller."

I knew right away he didn't mean physically, he meant in the Spirit. He meant that I would have learned to stand upright in the Spirit and in the Kingdom. I would have been better able to "see" the Kingdom of God. There is something about the challenging places—the outposts if you will—that makes it easier to connect with the Kingdom. Maybe it's because we're more desperate in this kind of environment. On the other hand, maybe Heaven actually is closer.

The Kingdom is Near

In 1972, shortly after I came to faith in Jesus, I was in Dallas for a conference. I was on my way to a meeting when I drove across a railroad track in a rental car, and the Lord spoke to me absolutely clearly. I still remember the spot where it happened and I still remember the word. Actually, it was a scripture, Zechariah 3:5. I don't know exactly how I knew it was the Lord, but I did, with conviction. As soon as I could pull over, I looked it up:

> 5 And I said, "Let them put a clean miter on his head." So they put a clean miter on his head, and they put the clothes on him. And the Angel of the LORD stood by. 6 Then the Angel of the LORD admonished Joshua, saying, 7 "Thus says the LORD of hosts:
> 'If you will walk in My ways,
> And if you will keep My command,

Then you shall also judge My house,
And likewise have charge of My courts;
I will give you free access
Among these who stand here.'[9]

Over the years I have seen that scripture fulfilled in my life many times and in many ways. One of the ways it has been most obviously applicable is that I have been called to travel extensively. In working for and with Anglican Archbishops, I have traveled millions of miles and been to almost every obscure corner of the world. It is hard to imagine how Christian leaders around the world could have been any more accessible. There has been "free access" to the leaders in many nations.

But free access has still meant a lot of hours on airplanes. Besides the ordinary rigors of international travel, there have also been times of stress and even learning to rely on God.

Just a few months after the Rwandan genocide, I was traveling by car from Bujumbura, Burundi to Kigali, the capital of Rwanda. Though we had reports that the way was safe for travel, once the road turned from urban to jungle, men burst out of the tree-line and surrounded the vehicle. Knowing that the *Interhamwe* rebels were still very much active, I knew it was reason for great concern. In the few days prior to our arrival, there had been reports of vehicles being confiscated and people being either abandoned or killed. So much for the reports of safe travel!

There was a great deal of shouting going on in Kerundi and French. I could tell from the French that they wanted the vehicle. I could also tell from the way they cocked their AK-47 machine guns that they were not used to being denied things they wanted.

---

[9] Zechariah 3:5-7

I experienced a jolt of adrenaline as the rebels approached the car, but there was also something else. There was a sweet, calm presence of the Lord. The Kingdom was near.

After the rebels yelled for a time, things seemed to calm down. And just as it had been in Iraq, all through it there was an incredibly amazing peace. The presence of the Lord was almost tangible. It was as though the Kingdom of God was kind enough to bend down to envelope us when we had need.

All the way on the other side of Africa, across the continent in Nigeria, under the despotic reign of Sonny Abacha, the nation was not unified in anything but the pursuit of corruption. In this one thing, there was mastery! It was all but *everywhere.* From landing to countless checkpoints on countless roads, it seemed like every government official, immigration officer, and cop had their hand out asking, "Do you have something for me?"

Nigerian Christians had warned me that there would be demands for bribes. What they told me to do about it, however, was simple. Scary, but simple: "Don't pay."

"If you pay bribes," they counseled, "Not only would you be adding to the corruption of our national soul, but spiritual power will drain out of your ministry. You won't even have to tell us; we'll know. But don't worry. We'll be praying for you." That advice was severely tested on three different occasions.

The first came just after landing. A circle of soldiers came up and surrounded me, pulling me out as the only white face in a group of arriving passengers queuing at immigration. There had been other western businessmen on board, but they had been scooped up just as they got off the plane. (A service available to those willing to pay off the immigration officials.) One of the soldiers, an officer, grabbed my passport and kept saying, "Your visa is not valid. You

16

have to have the original copy of the letter of invitation to Nigeria. You need to pay for a visa."

I knew they were scamming me because the written directions on how to get a visa had insisted that I submit the original letter of invitation with the visa application. We stood nose to nose for almost an hour. They kept saying the same thing, over and over, "This visa is not valid! You have to pay for an entry visa. We are being kind to you, we could deny your entry into Nigeria."

We seemed to be at a complete stand-off until a female officer walked up. She was obviously far senior to the ones who were attempting the shakedown, because they all stood at "boot-camp" attention. She wrenched my passport from the junior officer who had been holding it. She turned to them and said, "This is an important man. Release him immediately."

To me she said, "Come," and turned on her heel.

As we approached the exit, she handed me my passport and very kindly said, "Go in peace now, man of God. No one will bother you now."

After an hour of spiritual conflict and combat, I was stunned to see things break apart so quickly. I asked her, "How did you know?"

She replied, "When you walk in the Spirit, you learn to see in the Spirit. I saw your anointing. Go in peace now, brother."

On another occasion at the domestic airport, plainclothes police officers confiscated my passport demanding "landing fees." They were far less disciplined and not as sophisticated as the uniformed army bandits had been. They just began to demand money. Right out in the open, when I refused to pay their bribe, they began to roughly shove me and punch me on the arms. I only had the time to pray, "Jesus!" before two men called out from the crowd to the police. "Stop! He is a *reverend*. He is not some ordinary *businessman*. The Lord says in the Bible, 'Touch not my anointed and do my prophets no harm! You must let him go!'"

The police threw my passport back at me and walked away. God had arranged for those two men, who had been on the other side of Nigeria at a crusade where I had preached, to be at the Lagos airport in a divine appointment of deliverance.

On the third occasion of the hospitality of Abacha's regime, I thought I had arrived without incident. I had made it through immigration and customs without any problem and walked out the door of the airport rejoicing. My joy quickly faded as a military police officer and some security force men in civilian clothes took me by the arms and began to hustle me off into the darkness. Earlier on the flight, the Lord had given me a word of knowledge to have the phone number of the US Embassy in Lagos programmed into my cell phone on speed dial. I was certainly thankful for having the number available as I was being spirited away to who-knows-where. While we were still in the glow of the overhead lights I pulled out my phone and pressed send. On the first ring, imagine my relief to hear, "US Embassy, Lance Corporal 'something-something.' (I missed his name). How may I help you?"

I had seen the nametag of the leader of the group. In an instant, the Holy Spirit told me exactly what to say, "Hello, US Embassy. I'm calling to let you know of the wonderful service that this Nigerian police officer, Captain So-and-So has provided to insure my safety. I would like you to make a note of his name so that he can be officially thanked for his good service." Instantly understanding what was going on, the Marine at the embassy (the sharpest and the best Marines guard the embassies) said, "Sir, I can have a squad of US Marines there at the airport in less than ten minutes. Do I need to send them?"

"That won't be necessary, Lance Corporal. I just wanted to let you know of the *'good'* treatment I have received. Nigeria can be very dangerous. People disappear. I think it is enough just to let you know who it was who met me as I came out of the airport and *'how well'* he has seen to my treatment."

"Aye, aye, sir," replied the Marine. "Call us if you need us."

Confounded, the police officers had little choice but to thank me for being so gracious to them and let me go.

On each of the occasions there was significant danger, but it was not the danger that was my most poignant memory. It is the sweet almost tangible presence of the Lord right in the middle of deep spiritual conflict.

I have reflected on those experiences (and many others) a thousand times. At the worst of these circumstances, He was not absent but profoundly present. He was there in such a way that once having experienced His presence, I hungered for more. It is like worship, but more substantial--not just inspirational, but robust. Experiencing God's presence in that way was seared into my heart and memory.

Now, I long for it and look back upon it. It's like being homesick, even though it was only a moment in time. More than memorable, the experience of the Kingdom far overshadows the memory of any dangers. It has captivated my heart and I miss it when it is absent. Missionaries sometimes speak of something similar. Despite the dangers and the hardships of the front lines of mission work, it is a compelling place to be. It is as though the Kingdom of God bows down low from heaven and comes especially near the earth. It seems that if you stand on tiptoe, your head will poke through so you can get a clearer view of what Kingdom life is like. Once experienced, there is always a lingering homesickness to taste it again.

I theoretically knew that the closeness of the Lord with the aroma of heaven doesn't have to be restricted to the mission field or times of life-threatening crisis. There has always been the promise that there is more.

That is what is supposed to happen when Jesus heals us and invites us to abandon our hunched-over spiritual underachieving and He calls us to stand up to our potential. We break through into the new realities of the Kingdom. We come into a whole new set of rules.

That is redemption. We are healed so we can stand up straight. He wants us to live in the Kingdom of God. The rules are different there. Things are possible there, that should even be commonplace, that are dismissed as utterly impossible by the unredeemed and uninformed.

Conversations and wonderful teaching from a dear friend, Pastor Terry Moore, led me to thinking more and more about the Kingdom. Because of things I heard from him, I began looking up more and more Scriptures about it. Then a flash of inspiration came when I heard Bill Johnson, a pastor from California, talk about the Lord's Prayer. I had heard plenty of things about it before—I'd even used it as a prayer guide for years—but there was a new word in what I heard that day. "Thy kingdom come, Thy *will be done on earth as it is in Heaven.*" What I heard in that was, "The way things are in Heaven is the way God wants them here on earth. We are to yearn and pray and give our all for earth to be like Heaven."

Suddenly, I saw the Bible in an entirely new light. Scriptures about the Kingdom were all over the place. With wide-eyed amazement, I saw that Jesus came not just for people to be saved, but to proclaim the Kingdom. Parables and teachings were revealing the Kingdom being *here*. Of course, I believed in the Kingdom of Heaven. I had been thinking of references to the Kingdom here and now as being sort of a bridge or link to eternal life. There were even wonderful times when the life of Heaven had been manifested here. But suddenly, I started to see the call for the Kingdom to be established in our lives and extended through us. I saw more than just a responsibility to lead people to Jesus and disciple them; we are also called to proclaim and demonstrate the Kingdom in such a way that their lives are revolutionized and nations are changed.

The dominion that had been declared and experienced in the Garden was supposed to be re-established. The undeniable message of the Bible is the Kingdom. I was amazed that it could have been so plainly written, so desperately and obviously needed, and so compellingly presented and I had missed it for more than three decades. This was a revelation (and a *revolution!*) of the same sort of magnitude in my life as meeting Jesus and as experiencing the release of the power of the Holy Spirit had been.

It was utterly simple, yet unsettling in its profundity. In Heaven, there are no broken relationships. No sick people. No one is estranged from their family. No one lives under a cloud of depression. Palsied limbs have been made whole. Broken hearts have been healed, and sin does not have its way over anyone's life. Addictions have been vanquished. In the words of Isaiah:

> 1 "The Spirit of the Lord GOD *is* upon Me,
>   Because the LORD has anointed Me
>   To preach good tidings to the poor;
>   He has sent Me to heal the brokenhearted,
>   To proclaim liberty to the captives,
>   And the opening of the prison to *those who are* bound;
> 2   To proclaim the acceptable year of the LORD,
>   And the day of vengeance of our God;
>   To comfort all who mourn,

<u>3</u>   To console those who mourn in Zion,
To give them beauty for ashes,
The oil of joy for mourning,
The garment of praise for the spirit of heaviness;
That they may be called trees of righteousness,
The planting of the LORD, that He may be glorified."[10]

That is the Kingdom into which Tim was born. That is the hope to which we look. We have lived believing that there is a promise that will be fulfilled in Heaven, but the "reality" we have chosen for here has fallen desperately short of the truth. We may have slumped into the rut of believing that the power of sin in this life is so great that it drags the possibilities of the Holy City down to be a lesser habitation while we wait for Heaven. It may be fine to preach *"what will be,"* but we have lowered our expectations. Whether we are actually convinced that the stain of sin in *this* life is more tenacious than the redemption of the Church Triumphant or just act like it is, the effort is the same. Such thoughts may seem reasonable, and many people's experience may have borne this out, but imagine if they are wrong.

What if the victory of Jesus by which we will ultimately be made whole and holy could work here and now? What if the holding pattern of drudgery in local churches filled with people who are just trying to "get by" isn't in God's plan at all? What if He really meant it about storming the Gates of Hell? What if we really can disciple and change nations? What if we could actually address injustice? What if the Kingdom really is *here* as well as *coming*?

---

[10] Isaiah 61:1-3

Here and Coming
Here and Coming—Really!

In the field of geometry, there is an unusual figure called a Möbius Strip (or Loop). It was the discovery of Dr. Augustus Möbius, a 19th century mathematician and astronomer. He took a long thin rectangular strip of paper and formed it into a loop. Before connecting the ends, however, Möbius gave one side a half twist. The result was amazing.

What he produced and discovered is actually a one-sided geometric figure with a single edge. If you take a pencil and begin to trace along the surface, eventually you will cover "both sides" and come back to the mark where you started. This is without ever turning the paper over. The same is true of the edge. Follow along the edge and you will come back to where you started, but you will have also traversed the "other" edge. In reality, it is not the "other" side of the paper. It is the same side at a different place--really, really, weird.

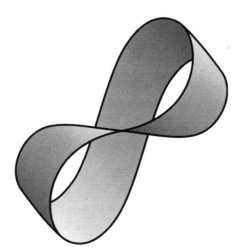

The wonderful image this presents is helpful in describing how God is able to hold two things in tension at the same time. As you look at the illustration of the Möbius Loop, you can see that what looks to be one side is actually the other, as well. What seems to be the top edge is also the bottom. What seems to be the "truth" or a "fact" at any point along the loop is overwhelmed by the whole thing.

As humans, we tend to focus on one thing and then another. For example, we can sometimes think of the demands of justice and another time think of the demands of mercy, but we can't hold both concepts at the same time. God can. The Möbius Strip (or loop) is the best example I know to demonstrate how He does that. He thinks differently than we do; He is different from us.

> "For My thoughts *are* not your thoughts,
> Nor *are* your ways My ways," says the LORD.
> "For *as* the heavens are higher than the earth,
> So are My ways higher than your ways,
> And My thoughts than your thoughts.[11]

If it is true that the Kingdom is *here* as well as *coming*, then we are no longer little squatty Lilliputian Christians, we now rise to a new destiny--Christians of full stature in Christ able not only to know His power, but also to do His bidding in the world.

While the power that works this miracle comes from God, we are not divorced from the process. His intention is so utterly gracious that He wants us to begin to take up his creative mindset and participate in the process of releasing His miraculous changing power. He has already demonstrated in creation that He can do it without us. He is just as clearly demonstrating now that His heart's

---

[11] Isaiah 55:8-9

24

desire is to work through us now. From the standpoint of the Kingdom, He is not showing off, but demonstrating and revealing the magnificence of His power. It multiplies His glory to be able to work through people.

A lot has to happen for things to begin to flow as they should. The process of turning us into ambassadors with power and a portfolio is far more challenging than it seems at first blush. It is a transformation that is only possible because it relies on the power of God rather than our own strength and insight.

We are not left in the dark comfortless without any guidance as to how we can become Kingdom-living people. There is a King in this Kingdom (Jesus), Who makes His dominion tangible and personal. He gives us power, and calls us to share in His purpose and to live passionately. He also gives us a roadmap. We may start off hunched over with a history of under-vision that has held us back until now, but we can break out of spiritual anemia. At every turn, He is revealing the structures, warp, and woof of Kingdom life. As the parts fit together, the Kingdom can come alive. Instead of being just the *Coming Kingdom*, we can start to see it as the Kingdom that is *Here* as well. It may be possible for human sin to sow a great deal of pain in our lives, and to even delay things; but the will of God cannot be thwarted. The will of the King cannot be denied. Things that stand in opposition to the principles of the Kingdom cannot last.

E. Stanley Jones observed:

> "...the Unshakable Kingdom, the kingdom of God and the Unchanging Person, the same yesterday, today, and forever, the Son of God is unique. And unique at the very highest. Never did the highest order and the highest Person ever come together before. And they

came together not by divine fiat or divine contrivance, but they came together because they belonged together, intrinsically so. We could never have understood the one without the other.[12]

We need to learn that we have received the Kingdom here and now. We also need to appreciate that we have the opportunity to meet the King. In that context, we need to learn to live and serve the King and His domain; for insight on how to do that, we turn to the Scriptures.

Receiving the Kingdom

Given the inspiring possibilities that God's Kingdom provides, it could be tempting to "get to work" to build it. But that is not the way of the Kingdom. Jesus makes entry into the Kingdom clear; it is through the Spirit.

> 5 Jesus answered, "Most assuredly, I say to you, unless one is born of water and the Spirit, he cannot enter the kingdom of God. 6 That which is born of the flesh is flesh, and that which is born of the Spirit is spirit."[13]

It has been common in some evangelical circles to describe this passage as *physical* birth (amniotic fluid) and *spiritual* birth (belief); but there is a wonderful quickening stirring among many contemporary leaders that sees not only the witnessing aspect of baptism, but also a supernatural component in it. That teaching—the historic position of the church—is being

---

[12] E. Stanley Jones, *Unshakable Kingdom–Unchangeable Person* (Bellingham, Washington, McNett Press, 1973.) Page 38.
[13] John 3:5-6

rediscovered in a powerful way. When people are baptized with the expectation that it will make a powerful difference in their lives, that is exactly what happens. It is clear in Romans that we die to sin in baptism and rise to new life (and new nature) in Christ.

Even though there is an *action* involved in baptism, the result of the process of conversion is really God's action for us to *receive* the Kingdom. It is first *received* and then comes the mandate for it to be *extended*.

> "But the saints of the Most High *shall receive* the kingdom, and possess the kingdom forever, even forever and ever.' [14]

While the passage refers to the *coming* Kingdom, it is equally true of the one that is swirling around us; even nearby, by the account of Jesus. How could it be less? If Jesus Christ is present in us when we are born of the Spirit, then His Kingdom *must* be at hand, as well. When He comes, He comes with all the outrageous magnificence of His other world that has been unseen to us but has not only been plain, but concrete to Him.

> "But you are those who have continued with Me in My trials. 29 And I bestow upon you a kingdom, just as My Father bestowed *one* upon Me, 30 that you may eat and drink at My table in My kingdom, and sit on thrones judging the twelve tribes of Israel."[15]

> "Do not fear, little flock, for it is your Father's good pleasure to give you the kingdom."[16]

---

[14] Daniel 7:18
[15] Luke 23:28-30
[16] Luke 12:32

27

<u>33</u> "Sell what you have and give alms; provide yourselves money bags which do not grow old, a treasure in the heavens that does not fail, where no thief approaches nor moth destroys. <u>34</u> For where your treasure is, there your heart will be also."[17]

Manifesting the Kingdom

"But go rather to the lost sheep of the house of Israel. <u>7</u> And as you go, preach, saying, "The kingdom of heaven is at hand.' <u>8</u> Heal the sick, cleanse the lepers, raise the dead, cast out demons. Freely you have received, freely give. <u>9</u> Provide neither gold nor silver nor copper in your money belts, <u>10</u> nor bag for *your* journey, nor two tunics, nor sandals, nor staffs; for a worker is worthy of his food."[18]

That is a far cry from the implicit (or explicit) message of many churches. They don't have much more to say than, "Please leave your check in the offering plate and don't leave the service until after the final hymn and blessing."

If we're honest, we will admit that we live in the tension of different experiences that may seem at odds with each other.

For example, Paul says "For we *were saved* in this hope…"[19] He goes on to say, "We are being saved…"[20] and then says, "We *will be* saved."[21]

---

[17] Luke 12:33-34
[18] Luke 10:6-10
[19] Romans 8:21
[20] I Corinthians 1:18
[21] I Corinthians 3:15

And this is where we live, in the midst of being *justified* and longing to be fully *sanctified*. We *are saved* but one day *we will be saved*. The Kingdom of God is coming, but it's also here. We are utterly free in Christ, but far too often live with bondages that seem to overwhelm us. We *have been changed*, but we also *will be changed*.

From the human, temporal perspective, we live in circles that overlap each other. From God's perspective, it is like the Möbius loop. Differing concepts that seem conflicting in human terms hold together in the heart and mind of God. We need to come in better focus with the Kingdom. When our experience doesn't line up with what Jesus says about the Kingdom, we need to root around and see if we can get our experience to line up with the truth. In the meantime, it's OK to say to God, "My life doesn't fall in line with the way You say that the Kingdom works. Help me come into the full inheritance of the abundant life you have for me. Help my prayers to line up with Your prayers. Help me make my life available for You to manifest your Kingdom fully." If we keep praying that, He will keep conforming us to His character.

Chapter Two
Three Patterns
The Trinity
The Eucharist
The Incarnation

Years ago, I was in my office reading the national newspaper from the Episcopal Church. In the Presiding Bishop's Easter column, he made no mention of the Cross, the Resurrection, redemption or any of the other classical Christian themes, but wrote that the modern church needed to "discover the holiness of homosexuality." It was a deep, desperate, and tragic failure because it robbed people of hope and healing. Jesus calls the church to offer a lavish welcome to everyone, but we are not called to stay the same. It is an invitation to become part of a body where we can become changed to be more like Jesus.

As I was reading, I felt something rise up inside me and I said, "Never again. Never again will I be silent in the presence of this kind of false teaching." Just as I was praying, someone came and knocked on my office door and said, "Jack Spong is in town and he's on the radio."

I took a deep breath and dialed the radio station.

Jack Spong is pretty well known for his ridiculous rejection of everything Christian. In his presentation on the radio program that day, Spong's theory was that we can be certain the New Testament is fiction because there are so many "stories" that were "copied" from the Old Testament. Because Elijah prayed to raise the widow's son, Jesus had to be shown healing a child. Moses fed the people in the wilderness, Jesus had to be shown feeding the five thousand.

31

There was, I explained to Kevin McCarthy, the radio host, another explanation. Instead of being fiction, doesn't it make sense that God would manifest His love and power in ways that have common elements if He is working over millennia? If *He* doesn't change through the years, wouldn't there be recognizable patterns to the way He works?

In fact, there are a number of patterns in the Kingdom that surface again and again, but three of them stand out dramatically:

The Trinity

The Eucharist (also called Communion or The Lord's Supper)

The Incarnation

The First Pattern: The Trinity
Three in One~One in Three

When God said, "Let us make man in Our image and after Our likeness," He was not saying that we *look* like Him. He was saying that we were created to *be* like Him. He chose to create and share His life—to live inside us. If we draw on the pattern of how the three persons of the Trinity work, then we may be able to get some insight into how Their various emphases work in our lives and contribute to the extension of the Kingdom.

God the Father, God the Son, and God the Holy Spirit are, of course, three persons of one God. All are equal and eternal, but they have chosen to emphasize complementary roles in what theologians call the "divine economy." That means that the Father, the Son, and the Spirit each minister with identity and purpose that is unified, but expresses diversity as well. Looking at the ministry roles of the three persons of God will be helpful in seeing what it is that we have been called to be and to do. Our ministry can be broader, and, hopefully, we can do a better job of fulfilling our potential.

The Role of the Father

God The Father has the place of being "the first among equals." Although the Son and the Holy Spirit are equally God, the Father is the One Who gives order and direction to everything. He is the "heart and soul" of creation. Creation is His idea; it is an expression of His life. The process of redemption is also the Father's idea. The Son and the Spirit work together with Him to accomplish His plan. When we think of "the mind of God," it is entirely appropriate for us to think of the Father, because of the role of leadership He plays. Of the many attributes of the Father, two that are most revealing are His love and creativity. As our Father, He demonstrates that love by giving us life and placing us in a world that is beautiful despite its flaws.

The concept of Fatherhood, however, was revolutionized by Jesus when He referred to His Father as "Abba" and told us to do the same. Rather than just being translated *Father*, the word would best be rendered *Daddy*. Imagine the magnitude of that. The ruler of the universe inviting us to call Him "Daddy." This does not negate the previous revelations in the Scripture about His holiness and His righteousness, but it does raise some issues. It is not enough to say that God is holy. We must also say that He is *compassion personified*.

The Father is filled with hope and encouragement. He is like Don Quixote looking at the fallen Aldanza and seeing the possibility for a fallen woman to *really be* "Dulcinea" (*The Sweet One*).[22]

Helpful Scriptures

---

[22] Dale Wasserman, "Aldanza" from "Man of La Mancha," (Random House 1966.)

Deut 32:6   Is He not your Father who created you?

Phil 2:11   The Son is magnified for the purpose of bringing glory to the Father.

John 4:34   "My food," said Jesus, "is to do the will of Him who sent me, and to finish His work."

2 Tim 1:9-10 All creation has been called to life to show the Father's glory, His manifold wisdom, and His creative love.

Heb 6:17   Through Christ we have seen the faithfulness of the Father's love.

The Role of the Son

God The Son exercises several roles. In creation, He is the "Living Word" who calls creation to life for the Father.[23] He can then be heard through the pilgrimage of redemption in the Law, and the word of the prophets (cf. Exodus 3:14 and John 8:58). In the incarnation, He shows us "God in the flesh" or as one six year old put it, "God with skin." The apostle John said, "No one has ever seen God (because He is a Spirit); the only Son, who is in the bosom of the Father, He has made Him known."[24] Jesus is God in a Body doing the will of the Father. The work of creation (and the Incarnation) is to show forth the creative power and love of God in physical terms. The Son's does the same thing in our lives by giving us ways to flesh out His life in our ministries.

Helpful Scriptures

---

[23] John 1:3
[24] John 4:24

Matt 26:39	Father, if it be possible, let this cup pass from me, yet nevertheless not as I will but as You will.
John 1:1	In the beginning was the Word, and the Word was with God and the Word was God.
John 1:14	The Word became flesh and dwelt among us.
John 4:34	My food is to do the will of Him who sent me.
Phil 2:6	Though He (Jesus) was in the form of God...(He) took the form of a servant.

The Role of the Holy Spirit

The words for *breath*, *spirit*, and *wind* are all the same in Hebrew. In Greek and Latin, the parallel also holds true.

Greek	Hebrew	Latin
πνευμα	רוּחַ *ruach*	*spiritus*
(*pneuma*)		

It would be just as legitimate of a translation to say "Spirit" where modern translations use the word "breath". It is also easy to see that there is a natural link between life and breath, since life departs when breath leaves. So, one of the main ministries of the Holy Spirit is to call people and things to life. We can see the effects of the Spirit, even if we do not always know how He works. But we can know with confidence that He brings energy and life to creation. His ministry to us is of that same character.

Helpful Scriptures

Psalm 104:30 When you send forth your Spirit they are created

John 14:16   I will pray the Father and He will send you another comforter/counselor (**παρακλητοσ** *paraklatos*) .

Romans 8:11 If that same Spirit who raised Jesus from the dead dwells in you, He who raised Christ Jesus from the dead will give life to your mortal bodies also through His Spirit which dwells in you.

Romans 8:26 Likewise the Spirit helps us in our weakness.

The effects of the Spirit are life-giving. He is *The Spirit of God*, the energizer, the One Who is the giver of life. And always, He seeks to glorify Jesus.

The Trinity of God

God The Father	God The Son	God The Holy Spirit
Gives Direction & Purpose	*Fleshes things out*	*Calls things to life & expresses Love*

Created In His Image

One of the greatest gifts that God has given us is that He created us in His image. Remember, rather than meaning that we physically resemble Him—that we're all tall and thin with straight teeth and lots of wavy hair—it means that we are made *like* Him. We share some of His attributes. God has given us the ability to create, to love, and to forgive. Even more significantly, He has made people in three parts, which echoes the pattern of His own identity.

The Human Trinity

The Human Soul	The Human Body	The Human Spirit
Gives Direction & Purpose	*Fleshesthings out*	*Place of life with God*

There is a fascinating parallel in the creation of mankind with the Trinity of God. Though there are many verses, especially in the Old Testament, that seem to speak of humans as unity, there are also many scriptures that speak to the human trinity. "The Lord God formed man from the dust of the ground [body], breathed into him the breath of life [spirit], and man became a living soul [soul]."[25]

All three persons of the Trinity of God are active in creation, and their creation bears the mark of their character. Trinity appears in us in **body, soul,** and **spirit**. Each part has a different role, and each part parallels one of the persons of the Trinity.

The Body

Everyone knows that their body is the physical and visible "house" in which they live. Our bodies are subject to "desires" of thirst, hunger, sleep, reproduction, etc. Seated in the human body are the five senses:

- •Taste
- • Touch
- • Sight
- • Smell
- • Hearing

While these senses prove to be invaluable in everyday living, they are not able to address the more abstract world of thoughts, feelings, and ideas. That is the role of the soul.

The Soul

---

[25] Genesis 2:7

The soul is the center of non-physical personality traits that reveal who people are. In the soul we find the operations of:

- Memory
- Reason
- Emotions
- Will

Basically, all the non-physical things that make *you*, "**you**." The computer age has brought about an interesting phenomenon. When people communicate via e-mail or with text messages, there are no facial expressions and there is no tone of voice. It is the soul that communicates. When you read a text from another person, it is rising out of their soul. It is very different from other forms of communication because it doesn't have all the additional information packaged with it that face-to-face conversation has. It is much easier for the communication to get derailed because the intended message is often not actually communicated. If you've ever had the experience of having a text message or e-mail misunderstood, then you know what I mean.

The Human Spirit

The human spirit should not be confused with the Holy Spirit. Originally, before the Fall, the human spirit was meant to be a dwelling place for the Holy Spirit and a place where we could meet with God. It was in the depths of the human spirit that fellowship with God took place. God was alive in the people whom He created before the fall and in fellowship with them. The human spirit offered:

A **dwelling place** in people for the Holy Spirit (residence)
A **meeting place** in people with the Holy Spirit (fellowship)

If we think of the human spirit as being like a balloon, a pretty good picture emerges. It was originally God's intention to live in us; that is, in our spirit, by "breathing" His spirit into us, and by meeting with us there in fellowship. When sin entered the relationship, however, it was as though the Holy Spirit fled, like the air from a punctured balloon. No matter how much God desired to have fellowship with us, this condition of a wounded spirit blocked that.

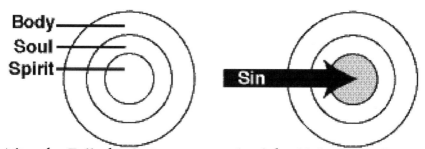

After the Fall, the Scriptures speak of the Holy Spirit "resting on" people, but they do not speak of Him *living inside*. That was the awful result of sin. However, sin is much more of an obstacle for people than it is for God. God wants us to be restored in fellowship with Him. The problem with us as unredeemed people is when He gets close to us, we want to run away because His holiness makes us feel uncomfortable. If we will just stop fleeing from Him and let Him embrace us, His love will begin to do its work. But, because we fear what the truth will bring, many of us continue to run—I know I did—and we flee with Him in hot pursuit.

In the words of Francis Thompson:

> "I fled Him through the nights and through the days, down the labyrinthine ways...and always He came...always after," like "The Hound of Heaven."[26]

---

[26] Francis Thompson, *The Hound of Heaven*. Nicholson & Lee, eds. (The Oxford Book of English Mystical Verse. 1917.) 239.

Every time I felt His breath, I redoubled my efforts to flee. Finally, He caught me and consumed me with love instead of the wrath I expected.

But we don't have to run. We can face the truth about our sin and rebellion and turn them over to the Lord to forgive and heal. In regeneration, our spirits are healed and called back to life, and the Holy Spirit becomes alive inside us. In a very real way we are changed to be "dead to sin and alive to God in Christ."[27] When we are alive in Christ, we are put into the same position as in the original creation before the Fall.

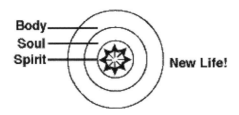

Life itself is a gift from God. The Son gives us the gift of new life (spiritual life or birth "from above"). The Holy Spirit calls us to Christ and then gifts us with power for Christian living.

Gifts from God

From the Father	From the Son	From the Spirit
Life	Ministry	Gifts and Fruit

In I Corinthians 12:4-6, we see a triplet of verses that describe how each of the persons of the Trinity are at work in our lives.

> 4 There are diversities of gifts, but the same Spirit. 5 There are differences of ministries, but the same Lord. 6

---

[27] Romans 6:11

And there are diversities of activities, but it is the same God who works all in all.[28]

• There are varieties of gifts but the same Spirit, (*N.B.*, The Holy Spirit gives us the love of God, and works through us with gifts that echo His purpose of calling things to life and expressing love, all the while, glorifying Jesus.)

• There are varieties of service but the same Lord, (*N.B.*, The Son gifts us with new life in Himself, then He gives us as a gift to His body for the purpose of ministry.)

• There are varieties of *workings* but the same God. (*N.B.*, The Father gifts us with life itself and an identity—a personality.)

Ministry Gifts

From the Father	From the Son	From the Spirit
Lifestyle	*Ministry Office*	*Manifestations*
(Romans 12)	*(Ephesians 4)*	*(I Corinthians 12)*

The gifts which each person of the Trinity gives are like the role that they fulfill themselves. The Father gives direction, the Son fleshes out life, and the Spirit calls people and things to life and expresses love. Their gifts do the same thing. A person's lifestyle is what influences the direction and purpose of their life. The Son gives ministry offices to the Body as His gift to equip and accomplish ministry. The Holy Spirit gives manifestations to Christians in order to express love and call people to life.

All three of the ministry gifts of the Trinity are important. In the past, people spoke of "going into ministry" as getting ordained and serving as a church pastor. In the last few decades, ministry has

---

[28] 1 Corinthians 12:4-6

been broadened for the members to see themselves as ministers who engage in ministry as a way to help the church. While that is a revolution, it doesn't even begin to release people's potential into the world beyond the four walls of the church. Focusing on the Holy Spirit's gifts, or manifestations, though a wonderful charismatic rediscovery, is not enough either. Those manifestations have primarily functioned inside the body of Christ. Even as robust of an image of church-life as it may be to think of an evangelizing body that exercises miraculous gifts, it falls woefully short of the vision to which we are called—to fully proclaim and richly demonstrate the Kingdom of God.

When the Biblical pattern of the Trinity is discovered, people can see that they are created for the Kingdom. The artificial distinction between things that are holy and things that are worldly has not helped. God intends that we should let Him reign in our whole life. Then, we are to take the whole Gospel to the whole of that life. The venue for ministry for each person now becomes not the church, but their life. Missionary endeavors are supposed to be rising from police cruisers, court rooms, offices, kitchens, hospitals and classrooms.

The role or emphasis of each person of the Trinity is supposed to be echoed in each Christian's life. If we are able to discover the way that the Father has knit us together, we can identify our motivating **lifestyle,** the **ministry office** to which we are called (both *in* and *beyond the body*)**,** and we are expected to remain open to the Holy Spirit's **manifestations** that the Lord has for each of us "as He wills." All three areas need to be released in order to discover our destiny to move into the Dominion to which we have been called. Sweeping action by the Holy Spirit is required if we are to fulfill our Kingdom mandate. As each of these areas are discovered and released, we will be called to a new way of *thinking*, a new way of *living*, and a new way of *loving*.

Discovering Your Motivating Lifestyle—"Who am I?"

Did you ever wonder why two people approach their lives so differently? It is because *they* are different. The key to understanding someone is not so much in finding out their *job*, as it is in finding out their *identity*. Their identity rises from the way they have been knit together in creation by God. It is very much like the Father's role in the Trinity. He gives order and directs how things will be done. The word that St. Paul uses in I Corinthians 12: 6 is ενεργαμα *energama.* It is the root word from which we get the word *"energy"*, what makes us *"tick"* or motivates us; and it is God's doing:

> Then the word of the LORD came to me, saying:
> "Before I formed you in the womb I knew you;
> Before you were born I sanctified you;[29]

Notice that it is God who says He formed us, and that it was according to His plan. He sanctified us. That means He set us apart for a wonderful and unique role. That life-force or lifestyle shapes everything we are and everything we do. It provides an overall approach to life that shapes who we are and it has a huge impact on how we think, feel, and act. Though it flows from God the Father to us, it is present in our *whole lives*, not just in church or church-related activities. Just as the Father is the directing force or the "soul" of the Godhead and the human soul directs much of what we do, ενεργαματον *energamaton* , is the shape a person's life takes or their motivating "lifestyle." The working, ενεργαμα *energama,* or "lifestyle," addresses who we are, how we see things, and why we do what we do. A person's lifestyle is an expression of their identity. When that is discovered, it is like opening a window into the "soul" of a person's approach to life and how that life can be released to extend the Kingdom.

---

[29] Jeremiah 1:4-5

Like the Father who gives this gift, it brings order and direction to a person's life. In the passage from Romans 12 that parallels I Corinthians 12 about ministry and the body, Paul talks about this same concept, "How we live and minister." In this passage, having already addressed the foundations of the faith, he goes on to talk about the attitudes and motives for ministry. Paul lists seven basic approaches to ministry, or lifestyles, that Christians have. These are perspectives which shape our whole lives. They are central to personality and the tone or direction of everything we do. When a person finds their "lifestyle," they will essentially be finding the "soul" of their life and the heartbeat that will shape their life into ministry.

> 1 I beseech you therefore, brethren, by the mercies of God, that you present your bodies a living sacrifice, holy, acceptable to God, *which is* your reasonable service. 2 And do not be conformed to this world, but be transformed by the renewing of your mind, that you may prove what *is* that good and acceptable and perfect will of God. 3 For I say, through the grace given to me, to everyone who is among you, not to think *of himself* more highly than he ought to think, but to think soberly, as God has dealt to each one a measure of faith. 4 For as we have many members in one body, but all the members do not have the same function, 5 so we, *being* many, are one body in Christ, and individually members of one another. 6 Having then gifts differing according to the grace that is given to us, *let us use them:* if prophecy, *let us prophesy* in proportion to our faith; 7 or ministry, *let us use it* in *our* ministering; he who teaches, in teaching; 8 he who exhorts, in exhortation; he who gives, with liberality; he who leads, with diligence; he who shows mercy, with cheerfulness. 9 *Let* love *be* without hypocrisy. Abhor what is evil. Cling to what is good. 10 *Be* kindly

affectionate to one another with brotherly love, in honor giving preference to one another; <u>11</u> not lagging in diligence, fervent in spirit, serving the Lord; <u>12</u> rejoicing in hope, patient in tribulation, continuing steadfastly in prayer; <u>13</u> distributing to the needs of the saints, given to hospitality.[30]

St. Paul calls us to the fulfillment of this kind of character in transformed living (Romans 12:1-8). He calls us to find out *who* we are, and then live out that identity to the fullest. He goes on to list seven different approaches to life, and calls each person to excellence in their lifestyle or approach to life.

1. For the **prophet**, excellence is found in faithful prophecy
2. For a **person of service**, in the quality of their service
3. For a **teacher**, in their teaching
4. For a person with a lifestyle of **exhortation**, in their exhortation
5. For a person whose lifestyle is to **give**, in the simple and distilled character of their giving
6. For those who **lead**, in their zeal
7. For those who do acts of **mercy**, in the good-natured quality of what they do.

When a person finds their identity in the emphasis of one of these seven God-given approaches to life (or perhaps in the mix of several), it becomes clear to *them* that He wants to play an active role in all that they are and do; not just on Sunday morning and Wednesday night. When a person sees their whole personality carefully knit together by God, they usually begin to experience a revolution that will release ministry beyond their wildest imaginations.

---

[30] Romans 12:1-13

Finding this ενεργαμα *energama*, motivation, or *lifestyle* also explains why two people approach the same ministry assignment so differently. Each of the seven lifestyles brings with it an approach to life as a whole. A person's lifestyle will shape every aspect of the ministry jobs that they do, but it will also shape their family life and what they bring to the marketplace. Each lifestyle brings a whole set of characteristics with it. Some lifestyles flourish in an atmosphere where a person can work with individuals. Some lifestyles work better in groups. Some emphasize relationships, others emphasize principles.

Our natural tendency is to expect that everyone else is going to think the way we do. When they don't, we are disappointed and sometimes we can even become irritated. Understanding the emphasis of different lifestyles can help us understand that others might just be *different*, not necessarily *wrong*. By tracing the Scriptures to where the root words for each one are found, an amazingly cohesive picture develops about each one.

Motivational Gifts or "Lifestyles"

Each person is created with an emphasis, perspective, or life view that shapes who they are and how and why they do things. When it is discovered, a person's "ministry lifestyle" becomes a comprehensive approach to life. It shapes how a person approaches any task or problem. People with different motivating lifestyles will deal with circumstance very differently and can have very different ideas of what "faithfulness" means. Every area of life is impacted by the motivational gifting we received from the Father when we were created. When people realize what their gifts are and how God has chosen to partner with them, it has a radical impact that releases ministry. No longer do people have to think in terms of "ministry" as teaching a Sunday School or even leading a ministry team at church. Now people are seeing that they have been created and gifted to share Christ in their workplace. Ministry can now mean teaching school, selling insurance, working in a bank, serving in government, or being a cop. It is a crucial part of extending the Kingdom of God into the whole culture.

A Prophetic Lifestyle

The word for prophet in Greek is **προφητειν** *profetein* . Its root meaning comes from its two components which are προ– *pro* for, φημι–*fami* to tell, utter, or say. Basically, this is a lifestyle of proclamation, but it may have non-verbal parts as well, as the person with a prophetic lifestyle seeks to bring order and direction to the community in which they live. The person with a prophetic lifestyle expresses love by challenging people to come to the fullness of their potential and to experience the fruit of doing what is right.

Prophetic people are highly verbal and unafraid to go against the grain of others.

A spokesman for others
Interpreter for God
Prophet
Seer

A prophet gifted for the expression of divine truth
Matt 14:5
Luke 7:15
John 9:17

Foreteller of the future
Matt 11:13
I Cor 12:28

To divine
Matt 26:68

Mark 14:65
Luke 22:64

To set forth divine teaching by a special faculty
I Cor 13:9; I Cor 14:1

Summary: This is a lifestyle **proclaiming** and **ordering** the community's life in accordance with truth, often through principles that have been revealed to them by God. For a person with a prophetic lifestyle, love is expressed by the intensity of their commitment and their desire for the community to do what's right. Prophetic people tend to be far more interested in groups than individuals, and more interested in purity of concepts than relationships.

Characteristics: Because the prophet is brokenhearted and indignant over the injustice, unfairness, and faithlessness in the world, their proclamation and call to excellence often reflects an element of sadness. The prophet loves people and focuses on the needs of the community, but will still unreservedly speak the truth with little or no regard for the consequences of delivering the prophetic word.

Possible Pitfalls: Those with a prophetic lifestyle can easily get caught by pride in their own righteousness and commitment, and can fail to rely on the Holy Spirit (i.e., they can trust in their own ability to persuade others). They are apt to be impatient with or insensitive to the needs of individuals.

A Serving Lifestyle

The word **διακονια** *diakonia* is translated as *ministry* or *service*, but it is also the root from which we get *deacon*. This is a lifestyle of concrete service caring for individuals. These are people with loving pastoral hearts who thrive in rendering service and caring for others.

I know of a young man who epitomizes this lifestyle. His name is Jim and he works for a railroad. In conversation over coffee, he admitted that he has always felt guilty because he is uncomfortable in "sharing his testimony" with other people. But that doesn't mean he has trouble sharing with other people. He thrives on it. Soon after seeing that he had a serving lifestyle, he stopped feeling guilty about where he is not gifted. He organized **The Holy Spirit Moving Co.** Most weekends, Jim recruits some friends to pack up household goods and furniture for widows and divorcees. He moves them lock, stock, and barrel when they have to relocate. No longer guilty, he glows when he serves and Christ's love is communicated when he does.

Matthew 20:26
Matthew 22:13   One who executes a commission
John 2:5,9

Romans 13:4   One commissioned with the gospel, a deputy

John 12:26   A devoted follower of Jesus or a Server

Romans 16:1
Philippians 1:1
I Timothy 3:8,12   One commissioned to distribute alms or to do
              other kindred services

Matt 8:15   To wait upon
Mark 1:31   To attend
Matt 4:11   To assist with the necessities of life
Luke 10:40   The act of rendering friendly offices
Acts 6:1   Relief, Aid

Summary: A serving lifestyle is one of **love for others** and a pastoral heart. Love, for a person with a serving lifestyle, is demonstrated in **concrete serving actions**. They are most comfortable with individuals rather than with groups. They tend to emphasize relationships more than concepts or goals.

Characteristics: The serving lifestyle demonstrates selfless caring for others. These servants of Christ are not interested in credit for work that is done. They are hoping only that Jesus will be glorified and that others will experience His love. They shun recognition. People with a serving lifestyle tend to focus on individuals and their needs.

Possible Pitfalls: Those with a serving lifestyle can easily get caught by pride in their accomplishments while thinking that they are better than other Christians who don't "do the ministry of Christ" to the downtrodden. Another common problem is failing to present the gospel verbally when it is appropriate.

A Teaching Lifestyle

Teaching in Greek is—**διδασκω** *didasko*. A person with a teaching lifestyle is one who unwraps truth so others can use it. The person with a teaching lifestyle expresses love by showing people what they need to do or how to do it. Naturally, there is a great deal of emphasis on learning so that they have things to teach.

Matthew 4:23	To teach
Matthew 22:16	To teach in public assembly
Matthew 28:15	To direct
Romans 2:21	To admonish
I Timothy 3:2	Qualified to teach
II Timothy 2:24	Apt to teach

Mark 4:2   Giving of instruction
Mark 12:38

Summary: In order to be qualified to teach, the person with a teaching lifestyle spends their life in **study**. They have a joy in discovery and they **learn in order to share** what they discover with others. People with a teaching lifestyle are likely to emphasize concepts more than relationships and connect with groups more than individuals.

Characteristics: They tend to have a steadfastness and joy in meticulous detail of study. They are able to enjoy long periods of time learning "with the Lord".

Possible Pitfalls: Those with a teaching lifestyle can easily get caught by pride in knowledge, resulting in being "puffed up" and "not seeing the forest for the trees." They can miss the life needs of the people around them while meticulously presenting details that are not helpful to those being taught.

A Lifestyle of Exhortation

A person with a lifestyle of exhortation has some of the same effects on people that the Holy Spirit does—a call to life, encouragement and hope. In fact, the Greek word is the same—παρακαλεω *parakaleo* , and it is the root for "Paraclete" or advisor. It is derived from· παρα–_call, and καλλεω–_along side. It |
is one who is invited or sent for. People with a lifestyle of exhortation have an encouraging effect on those around them that causes people to rise to greatness. They express love through affirmation and encouragement.

Acts 28:20   To call upon

Luke 3:18	Admonish
	Exhort
	Persuade

| Acts 2:40 | Beg on behalf of others |
| 11:23 | Beseech, entreat, implore |

Mark 1:40	To animate
	Encourage
	Comfort
	Console

| Acts 20:12 | To cheer |
| | To comfort |

| Titus 4:1 | Direct and correct |

1 John 2:1	One called or sent for to assist another
	One who pleads for another
	An advocate

| John 14:16 | One who renders beneficial service |

Summary: A lifestyle of exhortation *encourages and animates* the body of Christ. Exhorters are catalyzers who call things to life. They may be very much like a cheerleader, but are often more subtle than that. The person with an exhorting lifestyle has a clear sense of vision of the direction that God has for the community and they articulate it clearly. As they exhort, they express love by encouragement. They will exhibit their encouraging characteristics with individuals and with groups, but usually tend to be more interested in effecting change in a whole group, rather than being content to work with an individual alone.

Characteristics: Exhortation is a lifestyle of hope that tends to see the "diamond in the rough" in people. The exhorter is a person of prayer who often has deeply experienced the forgiveness and love of God in a dramatic way.

Possible Pitfalls: Those with an exhorting lifestyle can easily get caught by pride in the results from their ministry. Like Simon the Magician in Acts 8, when they see extraordinary fruit, it is easy to forget that it is "the Lord who builds the city." They can also fall into the trap of manipulating others for personal or financial gain. They can develop a deep sense of discouragement with other people who are not as quick to see God's purpose.

A Lifestyle of Giving (Sharing)

Those with a lifestyle of giving are the gift givers of the kingdom. The Greek term for giving, μεταδιδομι *metadidomi,* is a combination of, διδομι *didomi,* to give, and μετα, with. The implication is that this is a special kind of giving, a giving with *purpose.* There are several related meanings: to impart, to give, to bestow. A person with a lifestyle of giving expresses love by giving sacrificially with the hope that the love of Christ will be communicated.

Mark 13:11 To distribute alms
The manner of giving is described as: ἁπλοῦς *haplous* (simple).

ἁπλῶς *haplos* (*simply, sincerely, generously*) απολοτητι *apolotati,* it is a compound build from απο *upon* and ʽαπλως *simplicity.* The idea is "that which is built on simplicity" or "upon essentials." It is rendered several different ways in the New Testament:

- simple
- uncompounded
- sincere
- pure

53

- sound
- perfect
- simple, complete
- bountiful

Summary: Giving is a lifestyle that rejoices in **giving and sharing materially**. These are often simple people who give liberally with a joy and substance that comes from a frankness of character. Many of them know what it means "to be abased and to abound." People with this lifestyle tend to focus on needs rather than individuals. In general, they tend to be more interested in concepts than relationships.

Characteristics: Often entrepreneurs who are people with a lifestyle of giving, they love to make deals and turn profits in order to have the means to give. They delight in challenges and will work endless hours to reach a goal in order to meet a need. They delight in innovative ways to meet needs. They may well be simple, distilled and consistent people who give even out of their own need.

Possible Pitfalls: Those with a giving lifestyle can easily get caught by pride in giving. It is easy for them to fall into a pattern of materialism in their assessment of people and situations. It is also easy for them to fall prey to discouragement when the material provision they offer does not solve problems. They can be more interested in the need and the solution than the person with the need.

A Leading Lifestyle

A lifestyle of leading is one of supervision and oversight. The Greek word—ποιστάμενοι *poistamenoi*, is translated in several ways in the New Testament:

- To set over
- To appoint with authority
- To preside

- To govern
- To undertake resolutely
- To superintend
- To maintain the practice of...

As a noun it is used to mean:

- One who stands before
- A protector
- A patron
- A leader
- A champion

(Also see these scriptures: Acts 20:16, Acts 22:18, Rom 12:8, 2 Corinthians 7:11)

A person with a lifestyle of leading expresses love by arranging for people to get or receive the things they need.

Summary: Leading is a lifestyle of **accountability** and **protection**. These are people who have both a strong desire and a great ability to bring order to the community and to articulate vision. People with a leading lifestyle have a deep love for the Body of Christ and a desire to see it come to the fullness of its potential. To that end, they often seem more interested in groups of people than individuals.

Characteristics: They exhibit an earnestness and eagerness to serve God. They have a willingness to "stand in the breech" and take on the tough jobs. They have a willingness to be held accountable for the mistakes of those for whom they are responsible.

Possible Pitfalls: Those with a leading lifestyle can easily get caught by pride in their ability to follow God and lead people. They also tend to take criticism badly. Since they see God's plan so clearly, any criticism of the plan is seen as criticism of God's plan, or of God. They can also fall into the trap of exercising strong leadership to *drive* people rather than being sensitive to people's needs.

Showing Mercy

A person with a lifestyle of showing mercy (**'ελεων** *eleon*) will care for people with cheerfulness and kindness, not grudgingly. They seem to be unfailing in their ability to express compassion and care. There are several scriptures that are helpful.

Luke 1:54, 58, 72 Blessings
Rom 9:23

Matthew 5:7   To be gracious to someone
                 Merciful
Matthew 9:27   Show gracious favor
                 Pitiful
Matthew 15:22   Saving mercy or to be compassionate

I Timothy 1:13,16   To bring someone to obtain pardon & forgiveness.

A person with a lifestyle of showing mercy expresses love in ways that tend not to be concrete. It could be a smile, a word, a card, or a pat of encouragement that makes others feel better when they have been with them.

Summary: Showing mercy is a lifestyle of people with **gentle spirits** who love others and long to see an end to people's suffering. They listen tirelessly to the problems of others and exercise a healing influence. They are hospitable people who are never fatigued in giving.

Characteristics: Empathy and a sympathetic ear. They are the sort of people who join into other people's lives and "dance at weddings and weep at funerals." People with lifestyles of showing mercy have a healing effect. They tend to make people who are down feel better, though there is nothing "you can put your finger on" that was done to make them feel better. They are almost always more interested in individuals than groups of people.

Possible Pitfalls: Those with a lifestyle of showing mercy can easily get caught by pride in their sensitivity. They often exhibit an inability or unwillingness to offer "tough love." Because they are gentle and loving, they can consider their own lifestyle to be "Christlike" and they can dismiss others, becoming critical of other Christians who are not like them.

The Point--Who Am I?

The point of asking the question "Who am I?" is to get a window into how we have been knit together. When people see the hand of God in their lives moving in many spheres of activity, it is much easier to believe that they have been created by God to bear fruit.

Finding out *who* I am is a first step. As you pray over the lifestyles, asking God to show you which one (or ones) are most emphasized in your life, He will not leave you comfortless. He wants you to know. The next step is to listen and discern *what* it is that He has called you to do.

What Am I Called to Do?

When a Christian has begun to get some degree of understanding about who they are, there will likely be a new and excited awareness of the Lord's presence in their life. In fact, they will probably get quite fired up as they see the positive character strengths of *who they are* being revealed in all sorts of areas in their life. The more awareness a person has of the fact that their identity is a gift of God, the more likelihood there is that they will turn to Him for more direction. Different types of service are the ministries that "flesh out" or give hands and feet to the ministries of Jesus in and beyond the church. Just as He reveals the image of the unseen God, our ministry, or serving (**διακονια**—diakonia), reveals our character by fleshing out our identity. The appropriate question to ask is, "What am I called to do?" That question needs to be asked in all the areas of a person's life. What am I called to do in:

- My Family
- The Gathered Body
- My Workplace (Marketplace)

Imagine the possibilities of the people you know and love sharing Jesus and ministering in offices, in schools, in community affairs, and at home! Ministry in the gathered body is specifically listed as a gift from Jesus to His body (Ephesians 4:11). The ministry office in which a Christian engages will be an opportunity to "flesh out" or reveal *who* they are.

A big mistake at this point is to over-emphasize things that happen in and around church. While there are wonderful ministries that are carried out in the gathered Body, only about two percent of a person's life is lived there. If we are going to be effective in reestablishing the dominion Jesus has won through the cross and resurrection, we better be looking for the ways He wants to act in the marketplace, neighborhoods, and our homes.

Over the course of time it would only be natural to expect that the ministry office that a person fills might change. Their personality would not change, their lifestyle (identity) would not change, but the ministry office they fill might.

The temptation is tremendous to think of ministry as a series of activities in and around church. Christian businessmen are simply expected to make piles of money and give it to the church to fund programs. The idea that marketplace activities can be a launching pad to extend the Kingdom of God may have been forgotten, but it is true all the same.

Ministry offices will probably not change very often, but there is no reason to suspect that a person might have to remain in the same "job" forever. That is true when people are ministering outside church as well as those in marketplace ministry (even if it is not a paid position).

Ministry Offices—Gifts from Jesus to Accomplish Ministry

Paul describes a number of ministry offices in Ephesians 4:11-16. Ministries associated with leaders (who are often clergy in today's church) are His gifts to the church, for the purpose of equipping ministry in the lives of the members of the body. The ministries of the people include all the activities that support the people of God and all the activities that reach out into the world. But the Kingdom revolution does not stop there.

When people exercise a calling from God in the marketplace, it is equally *ministry*. It is the people who are the main source of *doing* ministry; the leaders are the ones who are supposed to be responsible for *equipping* ministry. Using the sheep and shepherd metaphor, the sheep are supposed to produce more sheep and produce wool. The shepherd is supposed to lead the flock to pasture and protect the sheep.

There is no need for the list of ministry offices in Ephesians 4 to be exhaustive. While many things are represented, there are others as well. It is no surprise, for example, that the Bible doesn't speak of a ministry of broadcasting or computer graphics. Instead, it is merely a representative list of ministry functions, with an emphasis on leaders' ministries. Paul lists:

1. **Apostles**—Apostles were originally the twelve disciples. After the death of Judas, they continued to proclaim the gospel, plant new churches, and offer spiritual oversight. Others were added to the company of apostles—first Matthias, then Paul, and others later.

2. **Prophets**—The office of prophet appears to refer to more than people who had spoken the Word of the Lord to the church. They were people who provided a kind of leadership that challenged people not only by predictions of the future, but by shaping the response of the people to address circumstance.

Acts 11:27 "During this time some prophets came down from Jerusalem to Antioch."

Acts 21:10 "After we had been there a number of days, a prophet named Agabus came down from Judea."

3. **Evangelists**—An evangelist is one who helps to lead others into faith in Christ. There are two types of evangelism—primary and secondary. In primary evangelism, a person shares the gospel with another and hopes to lead them to faith. Secondary evangelism is when a person brings someone else to a place where they can hear the gospel and be led to Christ.

4. **Pastors** and **Teachers**—Many scholars would agree that "pastor/teacher" is a combined ministry, since teaching is such a large part of effective leadership. There are other teaching ministry offices as well.

This list of ministry offices is representative of the types of ministry offices that are available to the body of Christ. Since the text says the mentioned offices are needed "to equip the saints for the work of the ministry," we should expect that there will be other ways to do that as time goes on. There are other ministries that are not addressed which are valid expressions of a person's lifestyle. A good example of that is music. Any of the seven lifestyles could be manifested in a ministry office of "musician" in the church. Depending on which lifestyle the musician has, the approach to the ministry will be different.

Manifestations—Expressing God's Love and Calling Forth Life

Lifestyles, or motivations, help describe a person's identity; ministry offices express or flesh out that identity. The manifestations of the Holy Spirit are called (χαρισματα) *charismata*. Remember, the ministry of the Holy Spirit is to glorify Jesus as He expresses love and calls things to life. Sometimes we will be able to do that out of our own resources and strength; sometimes that will not be enough. There will be times when we will need an extra gift of grace in order to communicate God's love.

It is primarily for this purpose that we are given the gifts of the Holy Spirit. They are gifts of grace to express God's love. The pneumatic (or *spiritual*) gifts are given by God and they are His possession. Even though they may flow through our lives with frequency, it seems inappropriate to say that we own them. If we had the same measure of control over these gifts, we would be able to use them as we chose at any time. A person with a teaching lifestyle will often be able to teach *anything*, not just about "spiritual" topics. That is not the case with the charismatic, or pneumatic gifts. If God does not quicken them, nothing happens.

The recipient of one of these gifts is the one who *receives* the answer, healing, direction, or the expression of love, **not** the one who delivers it. If you pray for me and I am healed, I received the healing gift. To most people who experience healing, the one who prayed is less significant than the healing itself. This puts the focus where it should be—on God—who gives the gifts, and their effect in people's lives. Since the purpose of the gifts is to communicate and express love, the atmosphere surrounding the use of the gifts must always be loving, or there is something very wrong.

In I Corinthians 12:7-11, Paul describes nine gifts, or manifestations of the Spirit.

1. Wisdom-*An extraordinary and supernatural solution to thorny problems which seem to have no possible solution.* One of the best examples of this is in John 8, when Jesus is confronted with the Pharisees who have caught a woman in the act of adultery. When they said, "Moses in the law commands her to be stoned, but what do **you** say?"[31], they were hoping that Jesus would choose His own teaching about compassion over the law. He would then be trapped into denying the Jewish law, and would, as a result, be branded as a heretic. Jesus' response was supernatural and complete. By saying, "Let him without sin cast the first stone", he fulfilled the law of love as well as the laws of stone.

2. Knowledge-*A supernatural gift, not naturally acquired in which information is given to the Body of Christ through one of its members.*

3. Faith-*A supernatural gift of extraordinary confidence, even certainty, in God's provision which is exhibited in such a way as to elicit belief in the lives of other members of Christ's Body.* The gift of faith is very much like a word of knowledge.

4. Healing-*A supernatural gift which brings healing of body, soul, or spirit through prayer which is given by God to an individual who is healed* (The focus is not on the intercessor).

---

[31] John 8:5

5. Miracles-*A supernatural gift which is an innovation on the natural order, which results in glorifying God.* There are two types of miracles:

- Signs σιμεον (*simeon*)-Which point to a person of the Trinity, an attribute of God, or to something about the Kingdom.
- Works of Power δυναμισ (*dunamis*)-Which demonstrate the sovereignty of God

6. Prophecy-*A supernatural gift of communication from God through a person.* A good way to think of prophecy is: "The mind of God expressed to the will of the listener through the heart of the prophet." When God gives a prophetic word to a pilot, it will probably be spoken in different terms than a shepherd would use, but the impact on people's lives could be identical.

Not everything that appears to be prophecy is from God. Some is real, some comes from the effervescence of human flesh, and although it is rare, there are also Satanic counterfeits. David Watson, a deceased English priest, offered this list for testing prophecy:

Does it glorify Christ?
Does it edify the Body of Christ?
Is it in accordance with the Scriptures?
Is it given in a spirit of love?
Is Jesus lord of the speaker's life?
Does the speaker submit to the church leaders?
Does the speaker allow others to judge the prophecy?
Is the speaker in control of himself when speaking?
If the prophecy speaks of a future event, is it fulfilled?[32]

---

[32] David Watson, *Disipleship,* (London: Hodder Christian Paperback, 2001)

Based on what we observed in those principles, there are three possible conclusions that can be reached. The responses that are appropriate will vary.

• In the event the leaders of the community judge the prophecy to be legitimately from God, it is always appropriate for the word to be illuminated, and for leaders to see that the life of the community is shaped to obey what God is calling them to do.

• If the word is judged to be simply coming out of the enthusiasm of someone's flesh, usually the best thing to do is to simply ignore it. It will have the dull nothingness of a lead bell and will be quite naturally ignored by the people. It is not usually necessary to make a big deal out of it. Honest mistakes that rise from the flesh can just be left to die on their own.

• On the rare occasion that the prophecy is judged to be a Satanic (demonic) counterfeit, that must be identified and the community taught concerning why this word violates the principles of the kingdom of God.

7. Distinguishing between Spirits-*A supernatural gift supplying knowledge about the source of a supernatural manifestation, whether it is good or evil.* We have confidence that the gift of discernment will *always* accompany the manifestation of any other gift, so we will be able to judge it with confidence. Even if the rest of the people don't seem to notice that something is out of order, the person (or people) who are spiritually responsible will either get a sense that something is out of order or someone they trust will raise the question. A person with unusual insight about motives and situations may be manifesting the gift of knowledge. The gift of discernment between spirits refers specifically to determining the source of a supernatural phenomenon so the Body can be protected from counterfeit manifestations.

8. Tongues-*A supernatural gift of speaking in a language which has not been learned and is not understood by the speaker.*

There are three distinct types of manifestations of this gift. Two are manifestations for the body and are like other gifts. The third is a private devotional gift that is given to individual Christians and may never be manifested publicly.

> • Acts 2:4-8 describes "other" tongues which were natural languages that had not been learned and yet were spoken by the apostles and others who were gathered together on the day of Pentecost. These languages were a dramatic sign for the "devout" men who were gathered in Jerusalem and were one of the factors that led to the conversion of three thousand people after Peter's sermon in Acts 2.

> • I Corinthians 14:5: Tongues with interpretation is described as being roughly equal to prophecy. It is simply a dramatic way for God to deliver a message to Christ's Body.

> • I Corinthians 14:4, I Corinthians 14:15, and Romans 8:26 describe a private prayer language for an individual's edification. When one *"prays in tongues"*, their spirit is edified (built up) even though their mind does not understand. Scripturally, there is no reason why all Christians could not receive this gift as an addition to their prayer life. In fact, thousands of people pray in this way and have never told anyone about the experience.

9. Interpretation-*A supernatural gift supplying the ability to interpret a message in tongues to the Body of Christ, so the gift of the message can be received.* Tongues with interpretation are virtually identical to prophecy. People who have manifested this gift often describe it as similar to receiving a picture in their mind's eye, which they share with those around.

The Church Unbound

Imagine, then, the church that would emerge if Christians were able to discover their identity and be released into their destiny to fulfill their part in proclaiming and extending the Kingdom of God, not only in the church, but also in their families, neighborhoods (*workplace* or other social structures), and in the marketplace. It would be time and energy well invested to help members of the Body of Christ find out who they really are and help identify ways that they can engage ministry in the church, although quite obviously most will minister *beyond* the church. It is a vibrant picture of a community of outreaching and transformation with the capacity to minister to the needs of the world around it, proclaim and manifest Jesus in clarity and power, and incorporate new members into the Body to be equipped to join in the work. No need could be so deep that it would be beyond the reach of God's love through the church, and no people so far away that they could not experience the love of God through Jesus Christ. It is just such a church that is being prepared as the Bride of Christ, and that which beckons us to come!

The Second Pattern: The Last Supper
Taken, Blessed, Broken, Given

Another great pattern of Christian life is found in Communion, also called the Lord's Supper or Eucharist.[33] Because this pattern includes the painful dimension of *brokenness,* many people miss the blessings that God intends. It may be disappointing, but the truth is that this basic pattern of life in the Kingdom must include the painful bits. That's not a guess or a theory. It was plainly spoken from Jesus.

> "In the world you will have tribulation; but be of good cheer, I have overcome the world."[34]

There is tribulation, but there is also joy. The drama demonstrated in the Last Supper when Jesus *took* bread, *blessed* it, *broke* it, and *gave* it to the disciples shows in a dramatic way (like the sacrament itself) how God often works. There is breaking, but there is also blessing. This pattern of taken, blessed, broken, and given is found throughout the Scriptures and it projects into Heaven. Of course, nothing is broken in Heaven, but that is the culmination where God's giving is most fully manifested.

Taking describes the action where people or things are set apart for Kingdom use. Theologically, this setting apart is called sanctification. It means we recognize that "this person," or "this thing" is being reserved specifically for God's purpose.

To be *blessed* means to increase people's understanding of the glory of a person or thing by recognizing the blessing that God has already conferred, or to call for a new one.

---

[33] **Ευχηαριστ** (*Eucharisto*) is Greek for "I give thanks" and is an ancient term for the celebration of Communion.
[34] John 16:33

Being *broken* is not the Humpty-Dumpty-shattered-into-pieces-now-its-worthless sort of brokenness. In the Kingdom, it is more like the alabaster jar of expensive ointment being broken *open* to reveal some treasure. No breaking is pleasant, but Kingdom breaking always reveals Kingdom treasure.

Once someone has been *taken, blessed,* and *broken,* then and *only then* are they ready to be *given.* When it is given, it is given to share fruit. The riches of the Kingdom are never hoarded. Like love, they increase when given away.

All through the Bible and Christian history this pattern can be seen repeated again and again. Look at the life of David--taken from his assignment as a shepherd boy, blessed in his anointing by Samuel (and no doubt in his victory over Goliath), broken as a result of his sin with Bathsheba, and then given for the ages in his repentance.

The same was true for Jacob, Peter, Saul/Paul, and even for Jesus. There is no reason to suspect that any other course awaits us. Jesus said,

> If anyone desires to come after Me, let him deny himself, and take up his cross, and follow Me.[35]

But He then continues on to let us know that it is worth it,

> 25 For whoever desires to save his life will lose it, but whoever loses his life for My sake will find it. 26 For what profit is it to a man if he gains the whole world, and loses his own soul? Or what will a man give in exchange for his soul? 27 For the Son of Man will come in the glory

---

[35] Matthew 16:24

of His Father with His angels, and then He will reward each according to his works.[36]

Our flesh hates it, of course, and tries to shrink back from the painful part. But then we are only shrinking back from inheriting the blessing that God intends. Sadly, the fear of the cost keeps some people from their destiny. While there is certainly suffering and pain that is not part of the process of "breaking," maturing disciples will gladly embrace whatever cost God requires, knowing that a magnificent harvest must come. It is the way of the Kingdom and ultimately will not be denied.

A great deal of modern "Pop" theology tries to shortcut any pattern that includes pain. Many of the post-modern theologians try to leap from *blessing* to *given.* In the words of the old hymn, "If you can't bear the cross, you won't wear the crown."[37]

The Third Pattern: The Incarnation
God becomes Flesh

After creation itself (which magnificently demonstrates the creative heart of the Father), the next most significant event that stands out in history to show us what God is like is the Incarnation.

The Incarnation (literally "to take on meat") is when God became flesh in Jesus Christ. Before that point (ever since the Fall) we were not in intimacy with God and couldn't experience Him as He really is. The effect of the Fall was to separate us from Him and from the experience of His love. He never stopped loving us, but we were so wounded in the Fall that we couldn't experience Him properly any longer. When Jesus came, all that changed. Now we don't say,

---

[36] Matthew 16:25f
[37] Johnny Cash, *Unearthed,* "Doo Lord," Disc IV, 2003.

"Jesus was a Godly man," we say instead, "God the Father is like Jesus." When you look at Jesus you see the Father.

> For it pleased *the Father that* in Him [Jesus] all the fullness [of divinity] should dwell.[38]

This was such a totally radical understanding of God; it took the church more than 300 years to figure out what had happened when the Word became flesh in Christ. Three hundred and eighteen bishops gathered in Nicaea. At risk was the future of the church because of disagreement over who Jesus was/is. St. Alexander from Alexandria held the position that the Father and the Son were of the same *"substance."* On the other side was the popular presbyter Arius, for whom the *Arian* heresy is named. He taught that the Son was not co-eternal with the Father. Through a powerful work of the Holy Spirit, the council overwhelmingly agreed that the Incarnation of Jesus was two natures in one Person. In His earthly ministry, Jesus was both fully human and fully God. Both natures are fully expressed in the One Person. There were only a few people (including Arius) who were unwilling to sign the Creed. What was remarkable was they wanted nothing to do with the church that produced it. Of particular note is the second paragraph which describes the Son and His ministry.

> We believe in one God the Father Almighty, Maker of heaven and earth, and of all things visible and invisible.
>
> And in one Lord Jesus Christ, the only-begotten Son of God, begotten of the Father before all worlds, God of God, Light of Light, Very God of Very God, begotten, not made, being of one substance with the Father by whom all things were made; who for us

---

[38] Colossians 1:19

men, and for our salvation, came down from heaven, and was incarnate by the Holy Spirit of the Virgin Mary, and was made man, and was crucified also for us under Pontius Pilate. He suffered and was buried, and the third day he rose again according to the Scriptures, and ascended into heaven, and sitteth on the right hand of the Father. And he shall come again with glory to judge both the quick and the dead, whose kingdom shall have no end.

And we believe in the Holy Spirit, the Lord and Giver of Life, who proceedeth from the Father and the Son, who with the Father and the Son together is worshipped and glorified, who spoke by the prophets. And we believe in one holy catholic and apostolic Church. We acknowledge one baptism for the remission of sins. And we look for the resurrection of the dead, and the life of the world to come. Amen.[39]

Now we don't have to wonder what God is like. How does the Father react to a woman caught in adultery, a repentant tax collector, or a rich young ruler? We know now. We see it manifest in the way Jesus related with them. If you prefer, you can hear it from the lips of Jesus Himself, "If you had known Me, you would have known My Father also."[40]

The amazing thing about the Incarnation is that it tells us that everything is going to be okay. When I was in college, before I met the Lord, I walked into a classroom where someone had written on the board, "Jesus is the answer." Underneath it, someone else had written, "Ah, but what's the question?" At the time I thought it was

---

[39] Nicene Creed 325 AD
[40] John 8:19

pretty good "one-upmanship," but over time, I decided that the first statement was correct. No matter what the problem, no matter what the pain, no matter what the situation, "Jesus is the answer."

When God takes the initiative to come into the world in the flesh, when you think about it, it means that everything is going to be OK. The Incarnation does not tell us exactly *how* things are going to be better, it just presents compelling evidence that it will all work out. If God is willing to go to such great lengths, it has to be for the benefit of His creation—for our benefit. Later, the Cross shows us how He works everything out; but the fact that He came at all is a huge encouragement that everything is going to be all right.

The wonderful thing about Incarnation is that it is not just something that happened in history. God taking on flesh in some sense is a pattern that is repeated again and again. Of course, the Scriptures are clear that Jesus is unique, but every time a person comes into a relationship with Jesus, He takes up residence in them. He has a new vehicle through whom He can manifest his love and demonstrate His power. They don't just become His follower or His friend, He actually comes into them and takes up residence. It is a diminutive version of God taking on flesh in Jesus, but it is far more miraculous than we give credit. It may well be that the earliest uses of the term "Christian" were intended as an insult, but there can hardly be any greater compliment than to be referred to as a "little Christ."

A third incarnation takes place when the church begins to come into its destiny. The Church *is* the Body of Christ. If we ever step into the fullness of what we are called to do and be, the world will see it. Like two sides of a coin, the way for that to happen is for us to pass through the Cross, both as individuals and corporately as the Body.

The pattern of Incarnation is not just found in the Word becoming flesh. It is also found in those who are in Christ. When we are born of the Spirit, a thousand things happen. We are born into His life and victory; we begin a great process of healing; we become inheritors of eternal life; and we become dwelling places for the Most High God.

> To them God willed to make known what are the riches of the glory of this mystery among the Gentiles: which is Christ in you, the hope of glory.[41]

Certainly, Jesus gives us hope, but there is ever so much more. Has anyone ever really embraced the *fullness* of what it means for Christ to dwell in us? Surely it is the very definition of magnificence.

Since the Church is the Body of Christ, then we should not only be acting like Him; the ministry of today's church should be indistinguishable from that of Jesus in Galilee.

> Now you are the body of Christ, and individually, members of it.[42]

Since we bear His name *and* have His power, "church" should look a lot different than it does. When Jesus walked into Galilean villages, He healed *everyone.*

> When evening had come, they brought to Him many who were demon-possessed. And He cast out the spirits with a word, and healed all who were sick, 17 that it might be fulfilled which was spoken by Isaiah the prophet, saying:

---

[41] Colossians 1:27
[42] 1 Corinthians 12:27

"He Himself took our infirmities
And bore our sicknesses."[43]

It's not presumptuous for us to carry on that work. Certainly it is authenticated if we pray for people who actually are healed and delivered. It is, instead, what we are commanded to do.

> 7 And as you go, preach, saying, "The kingdom of heaven is at hand.' 8 Heal the sick, cleanse the lepers, raise the dead, cast out demons. Freely you have received, freely give.[44]

If we really *are* the Body of Christ (and His word on that is surely true) then we, as the people of Incarnation, should act more like it. Why should this not be the age when we pray and *everyone* sick is made whole? Why can't every broken heart be healed and every bondage broken? Let's "do church" where every addiction loses its grip and every prisoner is set free. We are the people of the Incarnation. Shouldn't we expect to see more evidence of it? Don't brokenhearted people have the right to ask the ministry of the church to be indistinguishable from the ministry they would have received from Jesus in Galilee?

The more authentic we can be with each other, the more fruit there will be. It just cannot happen through the ministries of individuals moving through the earth alone. We must also gather together.

> If we don't grasp the intrinsically corporate
> nature of Christianity embodied in the church,
> we are missing the very heart of Jesus plan.[45]

---

[43] Isaiah 53:4
[44] Matthew 10;7-8
[45] Charles Colson, *The Body*. (Dallas: Word 1992) page 277.

Chapter Three
Three Laws
Sowing and Reaping
Binding and Loosing
The Triumph of Sacrificial Love

Just as there are patterns evident in the Kingdom, it also has a system of laws. Kingdom laws are different, though, from the laws of cities and nations. Human laws are easily broken. Often, the offense goes undetected. In the Kingdom, it works differently.

Spiritual laws are more like the laws of physics. One can *attempt* to break them, but the piper must be paid. For example, a person can climb to the roof of a building and deny the law of gravity. They may even write a detailed paper on their repudiation of it. If, however, they step off the roof, they will soon discover (in a dramatic and sudden way) that it is a law that cannot be violated. Kingdom laws are like that.

One may act in a way that is inconsistent with the demands of Kingdom law, but there is always, always, always a consequence. People who refuse to forgive find themselves in bondage. It is not just a punishment for a specific act of rebellion, it is the way the Kingdom works. There is no way to get around what God has established.

Law One: Sowing and Reaping

One of the first laws of the Kingdom is Sowing and Reaping. Just like the agricultural model described when you sow a seed, you reap a harvest. In the natural, when you sow carrots, you get carrots. Sow grain, get grain. In the Spirit, when one sows kindness, then some sort of kindness returns. Anytime we sow the fruit of the Spirit or the truth of the Kingdom, it will come back to us.

There is no guarantee, however, that we will receive back only the same sort of thing we have sown. This is because there are overlaps in the Kingdom. Attributes of the Kingdom share graces with each other. For example, sow kindness in Omaha and the harvest may come to someone you love in Detroit. Generously and freely give an offering to God and a broken relationship may come unstuck. The law is that when you sow in the Kingdom you will reap in the Kingdom, but we don't control how that will work or look.

Sometimes, there are specific additional promises like this one in Mark:

> Assuredly, I say to you, there is no one who has left house or brothers or sisters or father or mother or wife or children or lands, for My sake and the gospel's, 30 who shall not receive a hundredfold now in this time—houses and brothers and sisters and mothers and children and lands, with persecutions—and in the age to come, eternal life.[46]

The immutable principle that is manifested here is sowing and reaping. It cannot be stopped; it will not be denied. Millions of people live constricted, contorted lives because of the seed that they have sown. If bitterness is sown, bitterness will surely come back in abundance. Anyone who has ever had a seed-bed knows the harvest is greater than the seed. Plant one tomato seed and you'll get a vine. Plant rebellion and get hell on earth.

Again, let me emphasize here that there is a Kingdom; it is not a machine. Those who preach the so-called "prosperity gospel" are

---

[46] Mark 10:29-30

selling people (and the Kingdom) short. God has much higher priorities than making everyone financially rich. Even so, the Scriptures are clear that those who are generous financially will tend to have financial returns. When the return comes, however, there is a responsibility to invest, so ministry and mission increases.[47]

"Redemption and Lift"

It can be readily observed that those who commit their lives to the Lordship of Jesus Christ tend not only to develop spiritual fruit, but also to have a rise in socio-economic circumstances. Donald McGavran, often hailed as the father of Church Growth, described the process as "Redemption and Lift."[48] By that he means that there are blessings and benefits from living by Christian principles. They are so fundamental to life, that they bring blessing to those who live by them even if they are not in a relationship with Jesus Christ Himself.

This is directly observable in per capita income figures of Christian, Muslim, and Hindu nations.

Historically Christian Nations	$30,000
Historically Muslim Nations	1,000
Historically Hindu Nations	300[49]

There is some difference in the oil producing Muslim nations. In Saudi Arabia, for example, the small population has a per capita

---

[47] 1 Corinthians 9:8
[48] McGavran, Donald A., *Understanding Church Growth*, Eerdmans. 1990 Revised and edited by C. Peter Wagner.
[49] Dr. M. I. H. Farooqi, Gen. Secretary, Urdu Scientific Society, *Status of Muslim Societies around the World*, (Retd. Scientist (Deputy Director), National Botanical Research Institute, Lucknow)

income of $7,040. It is obviously a great blessing to have a country floating on a sea of crude oil, but that alone is not enough. Their income levels are still less than a quarter of those in societies built on Christian foundations. The laws of the Kingdom, like the laws of physics, rule over all creation whether people recognize them or not.

Judgments

There is another aspect of sowing and reaping that is so powerful that it could well stand as a law in and of itself (but that would mess with the way I've organized my outline presenting things in threes, so I'm including *judging* here). Of course, there is a harvest of pain to be reaped when we judge, so it is not *really* out of place.

Given that life is filled with judgment calls, what could Jesus have actually meant when He said,

> 1 "Judge not, that you be not judged. 2 For with what judgment you judge, you will be judged; and with the measure you use, it will be measured back to you. 3 And why do you look at the speck in your brother's eye, but do not consider the plank in your own eye? 4 Or how can you say to your brother, "Let me remove the speck from your eye'; and look, a plank *is* in your own eye?[50]

An essential part of God's life and character is not only to create, but also to declare the way things are. He speaks out of **ἐξουσία** *exousia*; power to act or authority. It is a compound word that literally means **ἐξ** *out of* and **ουσία** *being*. In other words, He creates and speaks out of *things that are*; things that are *true*.

---

[50] Matthew 7:1-3

When we judge, we are intruding on His divine office. Now, it is one thing to say, "That person is acting in a perverse way." It is entirely another to say, "That person is a pervert." One statement describes behavior, the other the essence of the person. It is precisely *that*, which we are not to do. Defining *who* someone is belongs only to God. When we do it, we are intruding on His office.

When we give up the right to make ultimate judgments on people's lives, it can really help us find peace. It also tends to help us be somewhat optimistic and positive because we don't give up on people. If we surrender the "right" to say, "So and so is a reprobate," we are actually expressing hope that their heart might somehow turn. The only one who really knows whether or not that is possible is God. Most of the time, He doesn't tell.

People's actions have consequences. Even when there is healing, forgiveness, and restored relationship, wounds almost always leave scars. It may well be necessary to restructure things to take that into account. For example, even if there has been repentance, it would not be prudent to put a convicted embezzler in charge of counting offerings and making deposits.

How then do we speak about (and to) those who have wounded us? Jesus gives the direction:

> 43 You have heard that it was said, *'You shall love your neighbor* and hate your enemy.' 44 But I say to you, love your enemies, bless those who curse you, do good to those who hate you, and pray for those who spitefully use you and persecute you, 45 that you may be sons of your Father in heaven; for He makes His sun rise on the evil and on the good, and sends rain on the just and on the unjust. 46 For if you love those who love you, what reward have you? Do not even the tax collectors do the same? 47 And if you greet your brethren only, what do

you do more *than others?* Do not even the tax collectors do so?[51]

Blessing those who have wounded and cursed you, instead of judging them, does two powerful things. First of all, it avoids the problem of intruding on God's role in their lives. He is the one who declares *who* they are. Secondly, speaking a blessing over them releases the power of God to work to bring about the best possible outcome.

This doesn't mean praying, "Thank you, Lord, for the wound that has been inflicted upon my life and for the bad thing that So-and-so has done." What it means is that we should pray:

"Lord, I commend So-and-so to You and to Your care. I pray that you will bring the best of your Kingdom to light in their life. I pray that you will help them find their place and purpose in the Kingdom and in You. I ask you to bring them into healing and complete alignment with Your will for their life. Lord, bring them to a place where their life is filled with the fruit of the Holy Spirit."

Can you see how everyone wins in that sort of situation? Whatever "satisfaction" might appear to come from having them severely punished will not bring as much resolution to our hearts or peace to our souls as having them line up with God's plan for their life.

Praying blessing over the lives of those who have deeply hurt us is pouring living water over a stagnant situation. Not only does the blessing start to bring healing to them, it spills over to bring healing to our hearts as well.

There is also another phenomenon. When we pray, despite pain in our lives, that costly prayer seems to have much more traction in

---

[51] Matthew 5:43-47

80

the Kingdom. Costly prayers have a special anointing to bring about transformation.

Law Two: Binding and Loosing

Bondages come in many shapes and sizes. They range from institutional or emotional bonds to spiritual ones.

The first congregation in which I served as a senior pastor was an old colonial church surrounded by cemetery plots of church and community members. The church building had been built in 1727. We used to say that the founders were still running the church.

One week, while some work was being done to refinish the floors in the sanctuary, the Sunday service was being held in the cemetery outside. *"Coincidentally"*, the Gospel lesson appointed for the day was the story of Jesus calling Lazarus to life from the tomb. Those words, originally spoken in a cemetery, took on a new dimension of boldness for me. As I stood by an old marble headstone and read the words that Jesus had spoken, I saw an interesting parallel with the story of Lazarus and the relationship of the Lord to the church.

His church, in the years after the ascension, has certainly taken on a different shape than it would have if He were present physically today leading it. It would probably be more powerful, and probably be more like Him. Despite that, we have to admit that staying here was *not* His plan. He chose to ascend, and chose to lead by the Spirit, through people. Mary's enjoinder, "Lord if you had been here, Lazarus wouldn't have died," was a statement of trust—and it was quite true. If Jesus had been there, Lazarus probably would not have died. It is also true of the church today. If Jesus had continued in His risen flesh to minister in the church, there are many mistakes that might have been avoided, and many places where the church fell ill, it might have remained healthier.

But it was not Jesus' plan to stay with Lazarus, nor was it His plan to physically stay with the church.

With the cry, "Lazarus, come forth!", Jesus called His friend back from death. In a similar vein, He has been calling the church to life in the renewal of the last thirty years or so. All over the world in unprecedented numbers, people are coming to faith and life, but the church is still not fulfilling its potential. A renewal of life is not enough—not for Lazarus, and not for us. Jesus told the people to release Lazarus from the grave clothes that were holding him back by crying out, "Unbind him and let him go." Even though Jesus had called Lazarus back to life, he was bound and unable to function in his renewed life.

Those words are equally true for people today, individually and in our corporate life. In fact, it is my sense that the prophetic word for the church for the next decade is "Unbind My Church to manifest the Kingdom of God!" Unbinding the church means to look at ourselves and our practices with ruthless honesty and to stop doing things that don't work or that inhibit the purpose of the church. We have had several decades to identify and remove natural obstacles that impede growth. In some cases, we have managed to build numerically huge churches, but some of them remain superficial and immature even though they are large. But there is ever so much more. God's desire is that we should reach everyone. That means that there will be bigger churches, but they must also be mature ones. That is not going to happen unless we disciple people in the Kingdom and adequately address the dark spiritual forces that bind and constrict us.

Our world-view shapes how we act. Many of the institutional structures that exist in the church were designed by default out of a world-view that assumes nothing of miraculous power or increase is ever *really* going to happen in this life. Some completely dismiss the possibility, while many others assume that we have to wait until the "streets of gold."

Being "loosed" also means being released from spiritual strongholds and principalities that all but smother Spirit-life and keep our witness anemic. It means loosing the power of God to heal and transform. It means living up to our potential in Christ.

As the charismatic movement progressed, it was common for people to pray to "bind Satan" or other evil spirits. Jesus speaks of this, but not as a parlor game. The binding of spirits should be accompanied by the loosing of the attendant reciprocal virtue. In other words, if something negative is bound and ejected, then the Holy Spirit, the fruit of the Spirit, and other virtues of the Kingdom need to be "loosed." That means that the good things need to be introduced, invited, and nurtured. Jesus describes the introduction and nurturing of good as "putting things in order."

> When an unclean spirit goes out of a man, he goes through dry places, seeking rest; and finding none, he says, 'I will return to my house from which I came.' 25 And when he comes, he finds *it* swept and put in order. 26 Then he goes and takes with *him* seven other spirits more wicked than himself, and they enter and dwell there; and the last *state* of that man is worse than the first.[52]

Anytime we pray against the assault of the enemy, we should also pray to loose good things like freedom, joy, and peace into the situation. Binding and loosing are not two different things. They are both part of the same process. When something is bound, something else is being loosed, even if we don't notice it. Lots of people pray to bind evil (or the evil one) and never pray to loose

---

[52] Luke 11:24-26

anything good. Consequently, they miss out on what God is doing and wants to do.

Anointing

In dealing with spiritual and supernatural conflicts, it is vital to understand our utter dependence on God. As He moves, there are people and tools God "quickens." The Biblical concept of quickening is called "anointing." The root in Hebrew is מָשַׁח *mashach* or to smear, anoint or מָשְׁחָה *moshchah* a consecrated portion.

When I was a boy, I used to love to go to my grandfather's place and work with him in his shop. He had absolutely the greatest stuff, the things of a boy's dreams. He had been an Army general and had been George Patton's Chief of Staff during World War II. He had Nazi daggers and swords that he had captured, pictures of famous people, guns and ammo, and the best tools you can imagine.

One of my favorite things of all was the giant round grinding stone that spun around when you stepped on a pedal on the floor. If you learned to time the energy from pumping on the pedal, you could get the sharpening stone spinning at a tremendous rate of speed. When it was spinning, we would sharpen anything with a blade and produce a magnificent shower of sparks. Before putting a blade to the stone, however, as it was spinning around, we would dribble "Three-in-One" oil onto the stone.

"Three-in-One" is wonderful stuff. It is used to loosen rusted nuts and bolts. A few drops on a stuck nut and bolt, and the frozen connection can usually be quickly released. When sharpening, it gave better contact with the stone. It helped the sharpening process, letting the wheel do the work of sharpening smoothly without having it grossly grind the blade of the tool to a nub.

"Three-in-One" is also great for lubricating things. Before the advent of WD-40, "Three-in-One" was in every toolbox. It pretty much lubricated every bicycle in every small town, kept every lock operating smoothly, and exiled squeaks from all manner of machinery. Anointing is like the penetrating oil of the Kingdom; it breaks bondages and releases the goodness of the Kingdom.

> It shall come to pass in that day
> *That* his burden will be taken away from your shoulder,
> and his yoke from your neck,
> And the yoke will be destroyed because of the anointing oil.[53]

Specific Anointing for Specific Tasks

While all who are in Christ have a certain measure of authority, wisdom is also required to know if there are special circumstances in which God wants to work. God's way and His purpose are always central to the situation. His timing, and the person (or people) who are anointed to minister in the midst of the task can be a critical component of how He wants to work. According to His purposes, God sometimes anoints specific people to pray, or specific ways and times to pray. Look, for example, at the conversion of Saul.

> Now there was a certain disciple at Damascus named Ananias; and to him the Lord said in a vision, "Ananias." And he said, "Here I am, Lord." So the Lord *said* to him, "Arise and go to the street called Straight, and inquire at the house of Judas for *one* called Saul of Tarsus, for

---

[53] Isaiah 10:27

behold, he is praying. <u>12</u> And in a vision he has seen a man named Ananias coming in and putting *his* hand on him, so that he might receive his sight.[54]

In a lovely example of Kingdom efficiency, God ministers to Saul and Ananias at the same time.

Sometimes it is important *who* prays. We need to be careful to know if *this time* is one of those times. Praying for the right thing is also critical to seeing fruit. For example, praying for physical healing when the problem is actually demonic will yield little fruit. The converse is true as well. When we are open to what God wants to do, He will lead us to the binding and the loosing that needs to take place.

Remember the earlier discussion about the Möbius Loop? We may see **binding** and **loosing** as two separate things, but God doesn't. He knows that whenever there is binding to be done, something is going to be loosed. In the same way, any time *something* is loosed, something has to be bound as well.

There is a story about a guy who is found staring at a thermos. Someone else is watching him. Finally he says to the guy, "Whatcha doin'?"

He replies, "Lookin' at the thermos."

"Why you doin' that?" comes the reply.

"Ya know how it keeps hot things hot and cold things cold? I'm wondering, 'How does it know?'"

---

[54] Acts 9:11-12

Anointing is like that. When we pray anointing on a situation (or actually anoint with oil), we are praying that God will release His Spirit to break the bondages that need to be broken and release His power. Creative bonds that build *koinonia* are also multiplied. Releasing *and* binding. Amazing. God knows what is needed and He will do it all if we will but ask.

From the beginning, we were not meant to be alone. We are called into relationships that will strengthen us and refine us. Sometimes, the refining process is a good deal sharper than we would like, but it can still be used by God.

> *As* iron sharpens iron, So a man sharpens the countenance of his friend.[55]

If we are wise, we will welcome this refining.

> Faithful *are* the wounds of a friend,
> But the kisses of an enemy *are* deceitful.[56]

When we allow the Holy Spirit to call relationships to life, God anoints them. Relationships that are anointed are like the precious oil on the head that binds people together in friendship and ministry. Look at what David says in Psalm 133.

> Behold, how good and how pleasant *it is*
> For brethren to dwell together in unity!
> *It is* like the precious oil upon the head,
> Running down on the beard,
> The beard of Aaron,
> Running down on the edge of his garments.
> *It is* like the dew of Hermon,

---

[55] Proverbs 27:17
[56] Proverbs 27:6

Descending upon the mountains of Zion;
For there the LORD commanded the blessing—
Life forevermore.[57]

The oil anoints fellowship so that brothers are bound together. Following that, there is a blessing: Life forever more. Real spiritual fellowship will lead to Jesus, and Jesus leads to life.

Law Three: Sacrificial Love Triumphs

> The oldest of the five Amish girls shot dead in a Pennsylvania schoolhouse is said to have stepped forward and asked her killer to "Shoot me first," in an apparent effort to buy time for her schoolmates.

> Rita Rhoads, a midwife who delivered two of the victims, told ABC News' Law and Justice Unit that she learned of 13-year-old Marian Fisher's plea from Fisher's family. What's more, Fisher's 11-year-old sister, Barbie, who survived the shooting, allegedly asked the gunman, Charles Carl Roberts IV, to "Shoot me second," Rhoads said.[58]

The shootings that broke hearts across the nation also proved to be the venue for glory to be manifested. The cynicism of postmodernism doesn't know how to relate to things like that. If they are reported at all, it is as a curiosity. Most of the noble things that transpire in today's culture go unreported. It's not really that they aren't news. The real problem they pose is that it's hard for a secular media to understand those kinds of sacrifices.

---

[57] Psalm 133:1-3
[58] Chris Francescani, "ABC Law & Justice", Oct. 5, 2006 .

Sacrificial acts like these arise from a living relationship with a personal God. The problem is that the actions of people who have been transformed by Jesus don't make sense to worldly people. | Meeting Jesus wreaks havoc with our experience and understanding! The empty tomb doesn't cast a shadow. It's more like a wonderful aroma that reinterprets everything. It's captivating, sweet, and more powerful than any wisdom or pain anyone else can dish out.

But, why does sacrificial love work so powerfully? I don't know for sure, but I can venture a guess. It works because Jesus did it. He demonstrated sacrificial love. It only makes sense that He did it because it was the only way. Sacrificial love is a free choice to offer life and love into a painful situation. It's like sending electricity into a situation that's stuck with dead batteries. It's like pouring water onto a parched flower. Sacrificial love is filled with creative power. It's when we become more excited about giving the perfect gift to the person whom we love than we would be in receiving something precious ourselves. It makes our spirit soar because we are resonating with the Father's heart. It is powerful and it works because it is made up of the same "stuff" that raised Jesus from the dead.

Chapter Four
Three Principles
Unless a Grain of Wheat
Be Humbled to be Exalted
Glory: Eternal things will prevail

Unless a grain of wheat...

Most assuredly, I say to you, unless a grain of wheat falls into the ground and dies, it remains alone; but if it dies, it produces much grain. <u>25</u> He who loves his life will lose it, and he who hates his life in this world will keep it for eternal life. <u>26</u> If anyone serves Me, let him follow Me; and where I am, there My servant will be also. If anyone serves Me, him *My* Father will honor.[59]

The "Grain of Wheat" principle is closely tied to the law of Sowing and reaping, and to the pattern of the Eucharist, but there are some additional Kingdom insights that it gives us. It's probably helpful, if metaphorical, to describe this principle in anthropomorphic terms, giving the grain of wheat some human characteristics even though it is not actually the case.

Think of a seed, knowing its basic purpose in life. It focuses on being a seed and celebrates its "seedness." Like a child that resists having to exit the womb or a person at the point of death struggling to stay in this life, philosophically, the seed wants to stay a seed. It has an identity and it has a purpose, as limited as it may be. The idea that it could have a more majestic purpose has never entered its "mind." It just wants to continue, and even celebrate being a seed.

---

[59] John 12:24-26

Locked inside, however, is a much more magnificent destiny. One tiny seed can give birth to many, many more. When the potential of the seeds that can rise from this one is also considered, it is even more impressive.

In order to get the potential out, however, something dramatic has to happen. The seed needs to be set in an environment (dirt, for example). Science channel time-lapse photography has shown how a seed waiting to burst will shudder and vibrate, and then split open to begin growing into a plant that will ultimately fulfill its purpose. It is not a death in the sense of an end to life, but it is a death of one existence in order to fulfill another.

The same thing is true of our lives. Locked inside is a majestic purpose and destiny. Before it can be released, however, a change must come that is so dramatic, the best way to describe it is death. It is not a death forever, though. It is dying to one thing to rise in another.

This can be easily seen in many areas. Take marriage, for example. The abundance of married life is infinitely richer than single life, but in order to inherit the riches of marriage, single life, its principles, and prerogatives must die. For a team to come to life, individuals have to give up some of their autonomy. Musicians have to embrace structure and limits in order to release the magnificence of a symphony. There is a death in the discipline. It's painful to give up the freedom to do whatever I want when I want, but the fruit of submission is tremendous.

Of course, Jesus is the ultimate picture of this. In order to release salvation, He has to lay down His life. When Jesus contemplated going to Bethany, He said to the disciples:

Let us go to Judea again." <u>8</u> *The* disciples said to Him, "Rabbi, lately the Jews sought to stone You, and are You going there again?"[60]

They didn't understand that he was not trying to avoid death. He was managing when and how it would come. For the disciples, schooled in what is called the "Orthodox Wisdom Position," they *thought* that the way the Kingdom worked was: "Be righteous and you will be blessed." Adversity in their understanding was the result of sin. There was no place in their theology for death or dying as a Kingdom virtue.

Jesus, on the other hand, knew how great the salvation was that would be released. He knew that the "seed" of salvation lay in Him and it couldn't be released until He had been dead and buried.

Our flesh is like the disciples in this point. It cries out to us, "Don't go to the place where you might have to *die*!" Little did they (or our flesh) know that they were providing counsel that would short-circuit salvation. Dietrich Bonnhoffer wrote, "When Christ calls a man, He bids him come and die."[61]

We are so much like the disciples in this. We want to find a way of having spiritual life without the dying part. In the sixties, there was a tremendously popular book about a seagull that was able to break through to heaven simply by *trying* hard enough. No cross, no death, no atonement, just blessing upon blessing. Fantasies work that way, but the Kingdom of God doesn't.

---

[60] John 11:7-8
[61] Dietrich Bonnhoffer, *The Cost of Discipleship*, (New York, Macmillan, 1959.) Page 99.

The concrete truth of it is demonstrated in the life of Jesus. When one considers the cost He paid for our sin, can you imagine that He would have done that if there had been *any* other way possible?

While everyone agrees that the crucifixion was terrible, most conversation focuses on the physical anguish. In truth though, as awful as the physical pain was that Jesus endured on the Cross, it pales in comparison to the literal Hell that He went through when our sin devastated His perfect relationship with the Father. We get something of a picture of it when He cried out, *"Eli, Eli, lama sabachthani?"*[62]

In heaven, God the Son had equality with the Father. But he was willing to give that up in order to share eternal life with us.

> 5 Let this mind be in you which was also in Christ Jesus, 6 who, being in the form of God, did not consider it robbery to be equal with God, 7 but made Himself of no reputation, taking the form of a bondservant, *and* coming in the likeness of men. 8 And being found in appearance as a man, He humbled Himself and became obedient to *the point of* death, even the death on the cross. 9 Therefore God also has highly exalted Him and given Him the name which is above every name, 10 that at the name of Jesus every knee should bow, of those in heaven, and of those on earth, and of those under the earth, 11 and *that* every tongue should confess that Jesus Christ *is* Lord, to the glory of God the Father.[63]

He died to bear great fruit. He calls us to do the same. For most of us, however, the dying is much less dramatic. What is encouraging

---

[62] Matthew 27:48
[63] Philippians 2:5-11

is that God sees in our character the capacity to empty ourselves something like He did.

In the film, "No Time for Sergeants," Andy Griffith plays the role of a bumbling hillbilly arriving to boot camp in the Air Force. In an effort to show how stupid and cowardly he is, other soldiers plan to throw a dummy hand grenade beside him in a crowded area. They expect to have a good laugh thinking he will panic and run, but are stunned when he throws himself on the grenade to protect those who have been nothing but tormentors. Everything changes as they see the courage and selflessness of someone who was willing to forfeit his life for their benefit.

> Greater love has no one than this, than to lay down one's life for his friends.[64]

Such a dramatic Kingdom act cannot fail to produce Kingdom Fruit. I know my life was changed forever when an Iraqi driver offered to sacrifice his life in my place. It made me not only appreciate life, it was a humbling example of the nobility that a good man could demonstrate even though he did not (at that point) know the Lord. Going through it also made me hungry to experience again the tangible, concrete presence of the Kingdom God gave as a gift, as soldiers had cocked their weapons to fire.

Be Humbled to be Exalted
There used to be an advertising slogan in Florida that declared, "The rules are different here."[65] What was posited as a PR slogan is unquestionably true for the Kingdom of God.

---

[64] John 15:12
[65] Department of Commerce, Division of Tourism, State of Florida, Serial Number 73626313, Filing Date October 22, 1986.

Across the USA, advertising expenditures for the first six months of 2006 exceeded $73 billion dollars.[66] That makes it pretty clear that American culture is deeply committed to the concept of promotion. The idea is that when people are told things are great, they will perceive them to be great. In the Kingdom, however, things work differently.

> ...he who is greatest among you shall be your servant. 12 And whoever exalts himself will be humbled, and he who humbles himself will be exalted.[67]

Jesus demonstrated this supremely in the incarnation. Theologians call it the "divine humiliation."[68] By choosing the humble path of human birth and entry into a stable on top of that, the Word of God made flesh has demonstrated one of the key principles of the Kingdom: exaltation rises from humbling. To make sure that we won't miss the lesson, Jesus plainly spells it out for His disciples. If we seek greatness we will fall. If we give ourselves over to the service of the Lord, His Kingdom, and His people, we will be exalted. The exaltation, however, will be in terms of the Kingdom, not the world.

"Why does it work this way?" you might well ask. Why is it that the One Who framed the universe would choose such a route? It is because He wants us to be redeemed. He wants everything on the earth, above the earth, and under the earth, to bow to Jesus as a matter of choice. He could force us to submit, but that submission would be empty. Fealty that is chosen is born of love. Submission that is forced is meaningless.

---

[66] TNS Media Intelligence Reports, New York, NY, September 6, 2006.
[67] Matthew 23:11-12
[68] Richard Bauckham, "God Crucified," Eerdmans, 1999. Page 70.

There is another reason, as well, that Jesus chooses the pathway of humility. Because Jesus has descended to a place lower than the least of us, then the most desperately lost among us can be redeemed.

I was speaking one day to the pastor of one of those huge "town square" Baptist churches in a southern city. He confided in me that he had caught himself lamenting that the only people who were responding to the "altar call" invitations were homeless people and derelicts from the bus station. With a good deal of embarrassment he said that he had found himself praying, "God, why don't you send me a more acceptable class of sinners?"

Jesus was not like that at all. He did not limit His saving grace to the upper crust layer of acceptable, white-collar sinners. The most depraved, the morally disfigured, the worst and most violent can be redeemed because He chose to suffer such utter humiliation. Many people find the manger less invasive than the Cross. If the truth is known, however, love that would choose to leave heaven's glories to be born into a stable is made of the same stuff as that which endures the hard wood of the cross.

We are at our most noble when we emulate the Lord's willingness to pour Himself out.

> Let this mind be in you which was also in Christ Jesus, 6 who, being in the form of God, did not consider it robbery to be equal with God, 7 but made Himself of no reputation, taking the form of a bondservant, *and* coming in the likeness of men. 8 And being found in appearance as a man, He humbled Himself and became obedient to *the point of* death, even the death of the cross. 9 Therefore God also has highly exalted Him and given Him the name which is above every name, 10 that at the name of Jesus every knee should bow, of those in heaven, and of

those on earth, and of those under the earth, <u>11</u> and *that* every tongue should confess that Jesus Christ *is* Lord, to the glory of God the Father.[69]

We are called to do no less.

Madagascar is a huge island off the coast of Africa. Most of it is undeveloped. The infrastructure is all but non-existent across much of its jungle. In many parts, there aren't even unpaved roads. One of the bishops who serves there is a tiny, gentle man with a huge heart for Jesus and for his people. Bishop Jean-Paul oversees a vast expanse of area, much of it utterly undeveloped. As we visited, I asked him how difficult travel was. He replied, "Interesting you should ask. I just returned from a visit to one of my churches that had never had a bishop visit before. Not once in the seventy-two years since an evangelist established a church there had a bishop ever gone there. There is no way to get there except on foot. It was one hundred and thirty-nine kilometers. It took four days walking." Then, with classic understatement, he continued, "They were glad to see me."

I imagine so.

The Weight of Glory: Eternal Things will Prevail
Glory and The Eclipse of the Son

The Kingdom of God is a tidy place. That's not because there is any paucity of resources or things, but because God created an orderly universe. The concept is called "Glory" (**δοχα** *doxa*), that everything has its place and "weight." Think of *doxa* like gold. Everything and everyone has a value attached to it.

To glorify something is to give it its proper weight. To glorify God

---

[69] Philippians 2:5-11

is to give Him a place above everything else. Temporal views on riches are at odds with the value that God places on people and things. Most of our "stuff" will be consumed in the blaze of judgment as time passes into eternity. The things that so many have labored for in this life are going to be revealed as insignificant, as we begin new lives of "seeing face to face."

Sometimes, we have a window into how it will be. Over the years, I have been privileged to be with quite a few people as they died. The conversations have fallen into two basic types depending on whether or not they knew the Lord. Those that didn't, wonder about what will happen after their death. While there may still be questions, those who are in Christ look forward to being with Him (even though they may have concerns with the process of dying).

Never, however (whether believer or seeker), has anyone on their deathbed ever said to me, "I wish I'd worked more. I wish I'd gotten more stuff."

Almost always they say that they would have had different priorities valuing love, friendship, and service over consuming, acquiring, and selfish isolation. As they are birthed into eternity, it is as though the refiner's fire strips away all the excess baggage in order to prepare them to be presented to the Lord just as they are (whether they are in Christ or not). Poignantly, even the most mature people who have done (what by all accounts appears to be) an admirable job of setting their priorities will often say, "I could have done it better."

In Kingdom economics, Jesus said, "What does it profit a man if he gains the whole world and yet loses his soul?" Yet today, many decisions are made based on keeping a tight grip on money and property even though doing so puts the souls of people at risk. Perhaps if we had a better grip on what priorities really are, we could do a better job of making decisions.

For me, the very best picture of glory comes from my two-year-old granddaughter. On a good day (and there are many), she loves to sit in my lap, look up at me, wrinkle her nose, lift her open hands and shoulders, and say, "Love you Granpa." She isn't looking for anything from me (except maybe a wrinkled nose and the hope for me to reply, "Love you, too, Brookie."). At some level, she understands that there is a glory about me that she wants to be around. At this point in life she isn't asking for anything in return. She just wants to *be there*.

When I come home, another devoted companion greets me with almost no demands. My Shar-pei (Chinese wrinkle dog), Mikey, greets me at the door twirling and dancing, delirious with joy that I have come home. My dear wife feeds him and takes him to the vet, but he bonded with me when he was a puppy. (I think he thinks I'm his mother.) He makes it obvious that it is his greatest joy and delight that I have walked though the door. Although this is a quantum leap, considering God's glory, we can be filled with a similar delight from knowing our heavenly Father and being with Him. Our delight is a reflection of His glory.

Fusion and Glory
93,000,000 miles away a barely controlled nuclear process called "fusion" grinds away squirting photons in every conceivable direction. The process of fusion involves two "parent" nuclei moving into one "daughter" nucleus. If you're interested in physics, the formula for the process is:

$$p + p \rightarrow 2\,H + e+ + n + .42\,MeV$$

where each "p" is a parent and "n" stands for a "neutrino." This is the process for unimaginable energy being released.

Unless the Lord intervenes in some way, scientists theorize that this process will continue producing vast amounts of heat and light until the hydrogen that is fueling it is exhausted. At that point they think that it will swell up into a red giant sphere that is so large it would overwhelm the first four planets that have been orbiting it (though it is a bazillion years in the future, in addition to the other problems this brings on, it means that the interminable road construction on Highway 75 in Dallas will have to be finished in the dark).

At this point, however, we are not so much concerned with the mechanism of fusion; rather, we are concerned with the Light it produces. Light reveals things for us. It not only gives us knowledge, but comfort. Remember when you were little and the dark of night made piles of clothes seem like unimaginable monsters? As soon as a light came on, the monster would melt into the harmless reality it actually is. Light can bring comfort and peace where ever it comes. Sometimes it brings conviction, but even that is in order to work out redemption in us.

Much closer to the earth, at only a fraction of the sun's distance, a lesser body exists with a goodly heritage. It is the moon. Its glory and purpose is to reflect the sun's glory and multiply our experience of the light. Stiff and lifeless itself, the moon moves with the earth. In its celestial role, the moon has given inspiration to lovers and poets. Despite the fact it is bereft of life or warmth, it elicits praise and fascination; and it does so even though it has no light of its own. Spiritually, like physically, it has its own glory. It exists to reflect the greater glory of the Sun, to brighten the nighttime and to remind us of The Light even when we cannot see It. The tides and romance are just added benefits. The church is supposed to be like the moon. It is there to reflect the light and celebrate the glory of the Son. However, when the church isn't reflecting Light, it becomes something dark and sinister, indeed.

Like the seductive Day Star song of Isaiah 14:13, the moral relativists of the day have said to The Son, "We have no need of You. We have no need of your Kingdom, Your rules, or Your Lordship. We have no need or desire of what you offer, but we desire what You possess. We will ascend to take your throne as our own. We will feast on the fruit of the knowledge of good and evil and decide for ourselves what should and should not be. We claim Your glory and will lord over whomever we choose."

There are two places where this can be seen with poignancy and clarity. The first is in the emptiness of the message of many mainline churches. While there may be pockets of light, the message in general is no longer a Gospel message. The institution has become its own message and messenger, and it blocks out the proclamation that it was created to make. The second place that reveals painful realities is manifest in the abuses of leaders who are attempting to hold crumbling institutions together with coercion. That is one of the most clear signs of the death of purpose in those churches.

For those who live in the Global South and regularly feel the tug of spiritual currents moving through their lives, the mainline church scene in North America has become utterly baffling. Conceptually, faithful Christians from other regions have trouble believing that this could ever happen in "their church." It is also why they sometimes seem to be naïve. When someone has had their life transformed by the Lord, it makes more sense to think that postmodern liberals will wake up than it does to believe they will continue to march defiantly away from Christ.

Postmodern relativism has woven the warp of presumption with the woof of arrogance into a new fabric that covers nothing. It has lost power and purpose. Significant parts of the church that were supposed to reflect the magnificent glory of the Son instead have maneuvered to make institutional life the center. It winds up blocking out the light and the life. Without the glory of the Son, the lifeless, gray, pock-marked lunar face has nothing to offer but despair and a hopeless future. Instead of being a moon that reflects the glory of the sun, the postmodern church has become a hindrance that is blocking the light of the Son. Those who live in the bleakness of the shadows will eventually find themselves shivering in the dark. Unfortunately, that eclipse isn't like the fleeting astronomical variety. Instead, it is a dramatic unfolding tragedy like a black hole that draws itself and those nearby deeper into the dark and into despair.

One of my favorite friends was Filipino Bishop, Edwardo Longid. He was the Bishop of Bontoc Province in the mountainous region of the Philippines. On one of his visits to the US, I drove him around for about a week. We had wonderful conversations and it was thrilling to hear his descriptions of things in the Kingdom.

One day, I asked him about a friend, "What would you suggest I say to a friend who is rebelling from God and running deeper and deeper into the dark?".

He only thought for a minute before replying, "Just tell him to turn around. If he is running into the dark he's going the wrong way. He just needs to turn around and face the light. He'll find the Lord there."

It was so simple, I had to laugh. For those who find themselves stuck in the dark shadow of the eclipse, remember, you can't move the moon, so we have to move to a different place where we can see the Son. We need to give Him and the things around us their proper glory.

Chapter Five
Three Purposes
Prophet–Calls to Life
Priest–Makes Offering
King–Exercises Dominion

Prophet

My earliest of all memories in life is of being carried around by my grandfather while he whispered into my ear, "Duty, Honor, Country." Those words were the motto for West Point, the United States Military Academy. He was a remarkable man and had a gift for calling things to life in the people that were around him. Born in Mississippi, he had to drop out of school when he was twelve because he had five younger siblings. He went to work in a sawmill in Mendenhall, Mississippi until all five had graduated. He didn't waste time, though. Studying hard, he was able to go to the University of Mississippi for two years until he got a Presidential Appointment to West Point. He graduated in 1917 and served in the Horse Artillery and then later, regular Artillery (those readers who served in the military might be interested to know that his service number was O-4444). He rose to the rank of General and became George Patton's Chief-of-Staff during World War II. He had a remarkable career. When he was blinded in one eye, a special act of Congress was passed to allow him to continue to serve with limited sight. When I was in college, he was in his seventies but was still sharp enough to tutor me in calculus.

He was a great leader and had a huge impact on my life. Of all the things that he did with me or said to me, none had more impact than the first: Duty, Honor, Country. To this day, I am deeply motivated to fulfill my duty. Of course, now I understand that more deeply than ever because it is fidelity to do what Jesus Christ calls me to do, but duty and honor are still the principles that motivate me the most deeply. I also have a great love for my country and my eyes easily fill with tears at the sight of a small town parade where people carry flags. In redemption, that translates to a love for the Kingdom of God.

What was active in the process of my grandfather teaching and leading me was the prophetic call to life. Good leaders and parents will find the truth to which God is calling those in their charge and will speak it into their life. The Kingdom doesn't work on magic, but there is great power when the God inspired word is identified and spoken into people's lives. Sadly, there can also be great negative power when the wrong word is prophesied over people, so we have to take great care to get it right. To function as prophets means to identify God's vision for a person (or people) and call that to life.

Priest

> But you *are* a chosen generation, a royal priesthood, a holy nation, His own special people, that you may proclaim the praises of Him who called you out of darkness into His marvelous light;[70]

In the Old Testament, priesthood was passed on through family lineage. In the New Covenant, the historic ordained ministry roles have been in the offices of Bishop (overseer), Priest, and Deacon. At the same time, there is a priesthood of all believers. It is the call on our lives to make offerings. There are two principal ways that we do it. The first priestly offering is when we offer things to God, before other people. The purpose is to speak the orderly truth of the Kingdom of the weight and way that things *are*. At the birth of a child or at harvest time we say things like,

---

[70] 1 Peter 2:9

"Hey, everyone, listen to this! 'Wonderful Lord, you have provided for us magnificently. We thank you, and we honor you, and we return to you from what you have given to us. Thank you, Lord!'"

The other way in which we make an offering is when we emulate Jesus, our Great High Priest, Who made an offering of Himself. Of course we cannot make an offering to atone for anyone's sins (even our own!), but we can lay down our lives in an offering. One of the most powerful witnesses we can bear to others is to lay down our lives in service or sacrifice on their behalf. However, the world doesn't function like that. Worldly concerns are to consume, acquire, and control, not to serve. When we act like priests and lay down our position, resources, desires, prerogatives, or even shed our blood for the sake of others, the fruit is tremendous.

Many people run from sacrificial acts fearing that they will be too costly. In fact, what we offer to God is multiplied. The price we pay for faithfulness always pales in comparison to the price He has paid for us. It always is. It's the law. And laws of the Kingdom cannot be circumvented. We may rebel against them, but they will have their way! Cooperating with the Lord of the Kingdom is the best way to experience the best fruit the Lord has to offer.

King
It is pretty obvious that God's plan was that He would be the King for Israel. But they saw other nations who had kings and they wanted to be like them. It is really tempting to rail against them and say how foolish and unfaithful they were to reject the perfect plan for green baloney, but it would be better if we don't, since we do the same thing. Jesus is supposed to be our Lord and the King of Kings, but all of us have rebelled against Him at one time or

another. We clearly demonstrate: "all have sinned and fallen short of the Glory of God."[71]

But we are called to do more than recognize and submit to Jesus as King. There are aspects of kingship that we are to emulate. While the priest is making offerings to represent the people to God, the role of the king is to bring the things of God to the people. We are functioning in a kingly fashion when we declare the truth about the King. The other thing that kings do is fight battles for their people. One of the ways to spot a good leader is that they will gravitate to the breach in the wall. They will stand in the gap. They will take on Goliath.

As leaders, that is exactly what we are called to do. Stand in the gap and take on Goliath. As the people of God and the Body of Christ, we are called to fight for those in the world around us who live without power, resources, or hope. When we do, the fruit will be great.

---

[71] Romans 3:23

Chapter Six
Three Battlegrounds
The World
The Flesh
The Devil

It was October of 1956 in Germany and already bitterly cold. My whole family gathered in the kitchen of the large stucco house to listen to the radio. The commentator was broadcasting from Budapest in English, but with an accent. The Hungarian Revolution was just hours old and the Soviet Union had responded with an iron fist. In the background I could hear the jingling rattle of tank treads as a vast armored column rolled into the capital to crush the rebellion. I was only seven, but I still vividly remember the grief I felt at the understanding that people were risking their lives with the hope of freedom and their hopes had been dashed.

Though my parents tried to downplay it, I was aware that soldiers from the Army battalion under my father's command were being sent out to guard our house during the night. I went to sleep that night with thoughts of soldiers, bullets, and bayonets.

The next morning I woke to tension thick as honey in the house. There were anxious conversations in hushed tones and it was obvious that they were trying to keep something from me. Desperate to know what was going on, I said, "OK! What is it!?!"

I guess they decided that disclosure was a better course than silence, so they told me what had happened. During the night an armed gang had rushed toward the house and the guards had to fire at them to stop the onslaught. There was an exchange of gunfire and eventually, the gang left. I was stunned. Imagine the horror for a seven year old. I couldn't even imagine anything worse. Of course, my parents thought I was upset because the house had been attacked. That wasn't it. I was devastated. A real gun battle had taken place *in my own yard* and I had slept through it. I spent the next several nights wrapped in a blanket looking out the window for "bad guys," but they didn't come back.

Years later, I discovered that another battle for the soul of the church had been raging and I had been sleeping through it as well. Normal sight and hearing don't work to identify spiritual conflict. A huge unseen battle has been raging.

Everyone has had the experience of days when things don't seem to go your way. We all know what it is to struggle and feel like things of the universe are "against us." The Scriptures are clear that "God is for us," but there is another awful truth. The devil is against us. He is the accuser of the brethren, the father of lies, and the thief. He sets us out on a path of seduction with the ultimate purpose in mind to control and destroy us.

The greatest tragedy in this conflict is that most people don't realize that there is a battle going on at all.

> The...eternal truth brought to us comes like a broken message over the radio, or an urgent e-mail from a distant country, telling us that some great struggle or quest or battle is well underway. Maybe even be hanging in the balance.[72]

---

[72] John Eldridge. *Waking the Dead* (Nashville: Thomas Nelson, 2003.) Page 28.

What is at stake is *everything*; the eternal destiny of people's souls. We need to get involved in the conflict, or bear at least part of the responsibility for what happens to them. There is no reason to suspect that this will be a pretty or lighthearted conflict. Even though many people surrender before ever entering the fray (or admitting that there is a conflict!) it is a battle that is worthy of our finest efforts.

> And from the days of John the Baptist until now the kingdom of heaven suffers violence, and the violent take it by force.[73]

> For though we walk in the flesh, we do not war according to the flesh. 4 For the weapons of our warfare are not carnal but mighty in God for pulling down strongholds, 5 casting down arguments and every high thing that exalts itself against the knowledge of God, bringing every thought into captivity to the obedience of Christ, 6 and being ready to punish all disobedience when your obedience is fulfilled. 7 Do you look at things according to the outward appearance? If anyone is convinced in himself that he is Christ's, let him again consider this in himself, that just as he is Christ's, even so we are Christ's.[74]

The Counterfeit Journey

We know that the devil is out to steal, kill, and destroy us and anything else of God's that he can. Rather than come after us with horns and a pitchfork, instead, like the song lyrics say,

---

[73] Matthew 11:12
[74] 1 Corinthians 10:3

"Lord, it's the devil. Would you look at him ... he'd have blue eyes and blue jeans."[75]

The devil is fully capable of presenting himself as an angel of light for a time in order to deceive people into their destruction.

As a result, he begins his seduction in the World. After all, it's really quite beautiful. What Satan wants to do is dip the values, relative morals, and standards of the world into the teacup of our lives so we will become steeped in them. He wants them to become part of the warp and woof of our lives. He wants us to watch so much television and so many movies that the insanity seems sane. He wants the once–thought–unthinkable to become the norm. Once the world seems ever so much more real than the Kingdom, we are on our way to destruction.

Worldly values resonate well with religion. The siren song is "Come as you are; stay as you are." There is a profound difference in the message of the Kingdom: "Come as you are and be changed." This message from Jesus is vastly different than the "consume and acquire" message of the world. His message is "It is better to give than to receive."[76]

However, if we don't watch our step, the wonders and glitter of the world can get our attention. The next step is to make it personal and begin to indulge our flesh. The flesh is where concepts and intellectual arguments give way to experience. At this level, you can be sure that the experiences will have pleasure aplenty "for a season."[77] The evil one wants to create momentum in our lives to diverge from Christ's redemption.

---

[75] Penny and Jerry Gillespie, "Somebody's Knockin," Single release, *Terry Gibbs, Somebody's Knockin*. 1981.
[76] Acts 20:35
[77] Hebrews 11:25

Battling the devil

The New Testament term for "religion" is **θρησκεια** *threskeia*. It is inherently something of a pejorative term in that it seems to rise from the root **θροεω** *throeo* to cry out (as if frightened). The idea seems to be that religion is a moving or even profound spiritual experience. Hopefully, maturity brings with it better behavior in the arena of religion. James points out that those who are religiously mature will be able to bridle their tongue.[78] He goes on to say that true religion **θρησκεια καθαρα** *threskia cathara* (literally *religion [that is] pure*) is evidenced in care for the fatherless and widows.[79] By contrast, *empty* religion would focus on oneself or seek to have God serve our desires.

Some of the devil's key areas of attack are listed below. Notice how readily they link with Satan himself or others of his dark kingdom.

To **steal**:	To rob something essential to life. Remember how Satan tried to rob God's throne. Note the contrast with Jesus who, as God the Son had "equality with God," but freely gave up His throne and the perquisites of divinity.
To **kill**:	To introduce something lethal–Jezebel
To **destroy**:	To control or destroy–Leviathan
To **deceive**:	To deceive and lead astray–Baal

James is very helpful in his instructions about battling Satan. He tells us to do two things.

> Therefore submit to God. Resist the devil and he will flee from you.[80]

---

[78] James 1:26
[79] James 1:27
[80] James 4:7

The first is to submit to God so we will be serving His purpose and agenda, and the second is to battle against the devil. To submit to God means to come under His authority and be "orderly." It is a compound word. ὑποταγή from ὑπο *hypo (over)* and ταγη *tagé (order)*. The Greek term used in James for *resist* is αντιστρατευομαι *antistrateuomai*, which is a compound made up from αντι *anti* and στρατευομαι *strateoumai (soldiering)*. We are not just to resist the devil, we are to *soldier* against him. We are to wage all out war to overthrow him and stop his assaults on the brethren.

The plan is sweeping and evil. At every turn, the fog of deception tries to confuse us so we don't see what is really at stake and we can be deluded.

> For false christs and false prophets will rise and show great signs and wonders to deceive, if possible, even the elect.[81]

On far too many days, a look at the news shows the tragic report of a key evangelical leader being caught in sin and crashing. How sad that the church has such an anemic view of the glory of God. It should be impossible to think that immediate, temporal sin-pleasures could have the exciting fulfillment of the joys of Christ! For that to happen, we need to plumb the depths of His love and power. "Lord, let me be lost in your love!"

> My beloved spoke, and said to me:
> > "Rise up, my love, my fair one,
> > And come away.
> 11   For lo, the winter is past,
> > The rain is over *and* gone.
> 12   The flowers appear on the earth;

---

[81] Matthew 24:24

The time of singing has come,
And the voice of the turtledove
Is heard in our land.

13   The fig tree puts forth her green figs,
And the vines *with* the tender grapes
Give a good smell.
Rise up, my love, my fair one,
And come away![82]

We are just plain rotten at seeing the things of the Kingdom. The influence of the world is disproportionate because we have so much more sensory input there. That doesn't make the world better, just "closer." It is as though the world is *shouting* and the Kingdom is *whispering*. Instead of being a competition of which voice is louder, we should seek to find our fulfillment in the pursuit of Eternal Love. That is where it really lies.

You will show me the path of life;
In Your presence is fullness of joy.[83]

The momentum of the world and the flesh are so strong, we need some other safeguards besides just keeping our "eye on the prize." Having some concrete expression of community in which we are accountable is crucial. Because we don't think in Kingdom terms deeply enough, it is far too easy to believe the lie that it is possible to "get away" with things. As a result, things are kept hidden and not exposed to the light. Unhelpful and destructive things churn away beneath the surface, like the awful, lethal mold that grows in houses until one day it breaks out and owns the dwelling.

A relationship of accountability where there can be honest disclosure of temptations is critical to maintaining our walk with

---

[82] Song of Solomon 2:10-13
[83] Psalm 16:11

115

Christ. Men especially need other men who will ask pointed questions about issues of integrity and sexuality. Without such support, it is hard to imagine how one might have victory over the onslaught of temptations that assault us these days.

That we are to contend with evil does not mean that we can be careless about how we do it. The natural tendency might be to "fight fire with fire." In other words, to give back to the devil the same sort of attacks and treatment that he is dishing out to us. The problem is, that will not work.

> Do not be overcome by evil, but overcome evil with good.[84]

In other words, don't try to fight the devil with his tools and methods, use the tools and righteousness of the Kingdom.

Instead of coming against the thief by trying to steal from him, we unseat him when we exercise *generosity*. Generosity is the fruit of the Spirit that is the opposite complement of stealing. Instead of trying to introduce something lethal against the evil empire (epitomized in "that woman" Jezebel) we undo the negative influence by living virtuously. Instead of struggling to gain control of others, we overwhelm it by submitting our hearts, lives, and agenda to God. Instead of the deception and falsehood of Baal, we commit to live by the truth.

Those who just try to grit their teeth and gut their way through temptation are very likely to fail. They fall because gritting one's teeth doesn't undo the power of the tempter. His influence needs to be undone, not shouted at. The way we win is through cultivation of goodness, not by trying to overcome evil by being the meanest son-of-a-gun in the valley.

---

[84] Romans 12:21

Jesus mentions that there are special circumstances that require prayer and fasting. It's not that we fast to impress God so He will move. Fasting is geared to help us.

We need to get spiritual conflict right because the stakes are very high. The farther along the journey we go, the wilier the devil will become. He wants to get us off track in our journey with the Lord. He knows that it will be really hard to unseat those who are far along the journey, but he will certainly try.

> For *it is* impossible for those who were once enlightened, and have tasted the heavenly gift, and have become partakers of the Holy Spirit, 5 and have tasted the good word of God and the powers of the age to come, 6 if they fall away, to renew them again to repentance, since they crucify again for themselves the Son of God, and put *Him* to an open shame.[85]

It is a sobering thing to think about becoming what we hate, but we had better beware that even though the devil is ultimately defeated, spiritual warfare is serious business.

Like the Journey To Be Like Jesus[86], the counterfeit journey is also a progression. Boundaries blur, then are crossed, then ignored, then ridiculed; finally they are attacked and destroyed.

At the same time, the conscience becomes seared, engages more slowly and less frequently, and offers objection more and more faintly until it is ultimately rendered irrelevant and replaced by the insatiable appetites of the flesh.

---

[85] Hebrews 6:4-7
[86] Bill Atwood, *Are we there yet? The journey to be like Jesus* (Carrollton: Ekklesia Society Publications, 2005).

King David's Terrifying Fall

King David sent his army out to do battle, but he stayed behind in Jerusalem.[87] From his palace, he saw a beautiful woman bathing. Indulging himself, he sent for her, slept with her and sent her home. Not long after, he learned that the liaison had conceived a child.

Now, David was Israel's king and by their standards entitled to take a wife – more than one, if he fancied. But somewhere along the line his boundaries began to get foggy, and he dramatically crossed the line by taking another man's wife. Having sinned with her and gotten her pregnant, his conscience was seared and started to atrophy. He tried to cover it up by calling Bathsheba's husband, Uriah, back from the battle in the hope that Uriah would sleep with his wife and no one would be the wiser. But the plan failed. Uriah was not willing to indulge in pleasure for himself while his troops were at war. In desperation, David trampled any sensible boundaries and had Uriah killed.

"But God..." what wonderful words. "But God Who is rich in mercy"[88] had compassion on King David and sent the prophet Nathan to prick the king's conscience and try to goad it to life.[89] In this case, because David had "a heart after God's own heart," [90] he collapsed in repentance and was ultimately restored. Sadly, sin still exacted its temporal consequences in his life.[91]

---

[87] 2 Samuel 11-12
[88] Ephesians 2:4
[89] 2 Samuel 12:7
[90] 1 Samuel 13:14
[91] 2 Samuel 12:7

The Perils of Post–Modernity

There are amazing parallels between the journeys of the modern day post-modern liberal denominational leaders and the Pharisees. Obviously any comparison with the Pharisees will be seen as pejorative; but the process of blurring, then transgressing historic boundaries is virtually identical.

First, boundaries were blurred.

> 1 Then the scribes and Pharisees who were from Jerusalem came to Jesus, saying, 2 "Why do Your disciples transgress the tradition of the elders? For they do not wash their hands when they eat bread." 3 He answered and said to them, "Why do you also transgress the commandment of God because of your tradition? 4 For God commanded, saying, *'Honor your father and your mother'*; and, *'He who curses father or mother, let him be put to death.'* 5 But you say, 'Whoever says to his father or mother, "Whatever profit you might have received from me *is* a gift *to God"*— 6 then he need not honor his father or mother.' Thus you have made the commandment of God of no effect by your tradition.[92]

Then crossed.

> Then Jesus spoke to the multitudes and to His disciples, saying: "The scribes and the Pharisees sit in Moses' seat. Therefore whatever they tell you to observe, *that* observe and do, but do not do according to their works; for they say, and do not do.[93]

---

[92] Matthew 15:1-6
[93] Matthew 23:1-3

Ignored.

> "Woe to you, scribes and Pharisees, hypocrites! For you pay tithe of mint and anise and cummin, and have neglected the weightier matters of the law: justice and mercy and faith. These you ought to have done, without leaving the others undone.

Ridiculed.

> Likewise the chief priests also, mocking with the scribes and elders, said, "He saved others; Himself He cannot save. If He is the King of Israel, let Him now come down from the cross, and we will believe Him. He trusted in God; let Him deliver Him now if He will have Him; for He said, 'I am the Son of God.'"[94]

Attacked and destroyed.

> Then the Pharisees went out and plotted against Him, how they might destroy Him.[95]

It is a terrifying thing to realize that what starts as a simple moral stroll, thinking that it won't matter all that much if we cross this boundary or that, can lead to disaster. If we continue down the road of moral compromise, it won't be long before we rationalize our way into serious trouble. Ultimately, we can wind up joining in the warfare against the Kingdom and the King.

---

[94] Matthew 27:41-43
[95] Matthew 12:14

Three Leavens

The classic enemies of the church are the world, the flesh, and the devil. They represent three spheres of a descent into rebellion, ultimately resulting in eternal separation from Christ. Jesus speaks about this kind of danger:

> Then He charged them, saying, "Take heed, beware of the leaven of the Pharisees and the leaven of Herod."[96]

and

> "...beware of the leaven of the Pharisees and Sadducees."[97]

He cites three different types of leaven:

> The Leaven of The Sadducees
> The Leaven of The Pharisees
> The Leaven of Herod

Leaven is the stuff you add to flour to make the dough rise. A little of it is all that is necessary to bring about tremendous transformation. In the case of bread, it is a positive change. In the case of the leaven of the Pharisees, the Sadducees, and Herod, it is change for great ill.

Jesus wasn't clear about exactly and specifically what He meant by the image, but there are some things we can say about these various "leavens."

---

[96] Mark 8:14
[97] Matthew 16:11

The Sadducees were influenced by the world. They especially didn't like the supernatural. They did not believe in the resurrection (...and that is why they were "sad...you see?").[98] Their leaven is the leaven of the world. The more we steep in the values and priorities of the world, the more they will influence and stain us. Many of our "liberal" friends have fallen prey to the mindset of the world. There is little to differentiate the thinking of the modern day ecclesiastical Sadducees from the leaders of secular society. The leaven of the Sadducees is not the thing that will likely influence conservatives, but it is worth a mention.

The leaven of Herod is a more serious threat for those of us who are conservative. It reminds us of the flesh. Remember how Herod wanted to be (as *The Best Christmas Pageant Ever* describes) "the main king"?[99] He was a flesh-fest for sure. He indulged himself and sought power so ruthlessly he killed all the children under two years old (the Holy Innocents) in order to try to eliminate the Messiah. While our behavior is usually more subtle, the heart of what he did is far too easy to own. When we try to maneuver events to build up our personal empire, we open the door to the Leaven of Herod. Just like with yeast in bread, it doesn't take much to introduce a huge problem that can be not only damaging, but exhausting. A pentecostal preacher I heard once said, "I don't want to build nuthin' in the flesh 'cuz then I'd have to maintain it in my own strength."

As principled conservatives, we also run the risk of being like the Pharisees: persnickety and loveless. Eventually, Pharisees become so bitter and dark they begin to mirror the evil one himself. Jesus said it gently, "You are of your father, the devil!" The Pharisees

---

[98] Matthew 22:23
[99] Barbara Robinson, *The Best Christmas Pageant Ever* (Harper Trophy Waco 1972) Page 53.

focused so ardently on the details they missed the point of the whole process.

While it is easier to see the flaws in other conservatives, it would behoove us to give a good and critical eye to our own hearts and lives. We can preserve distinctives without indulging in separatism, but the temptation is strong to live less nobly. When things are breaking up around us, isn't that the time to strive for doctrinal purity? I mean, if we are going to have to live through upheaval, why not pay the price to get it *all* right? Why not cut ourselves off from all those who fall short? Why not use the opportunity to separate from everyone whose theology is flawed in any way? We may not want to admit it, but the temptation is huge to act like that. Once fracturing begins, its natural tendency is to splinter and spread until we are all but alone in our purity. It is critically important for us to discern what are essential things and what are in the category of, αδιαπηορα *adiaphora* (non-essentials).

> The question then naturally arises as to how one can tell, and indeed as to who can decide, which types of behaviour count as 'adiaphora' and which do not. For Paul, the categories are not arbitrary, but clearly distinct. For instance: that which would otherwise separate Jew and Gentile within the Church is 'adiaphora'. That which embodies and expresses renewed humanity in Christ is always mandatory for Christians; that which embodies the dehumanising turning-away-from-God which Paul characterises with such terms as 'sin', 'flesh', and so on, is always forbidden.[100]

---

[100] Robin Eames (Abp), et al, *The Lambeth Commission on Communion* (Anglican Communion London 2004), Page 10.

Of course, The Bible is the place to look for clarity about essentials! When there is conflict there are better ways to deal with it than through unnecessary fracturing. Recently, one of the East African Archbishops said to me, "We are all sons of the East African Revival. When we bog down and get stuck, someone will say, 'Remember we are all sons of the Revival,' and everyone will stop and nod and the atmosphere will change. We will start working together again and pray to find agreement where we can and charity where we disagree." We could learn from that. If we don't the leaven of the Pharisees could assault us with vengeance.

The real solution in this, however, is not just to try to avoid pitfalls. We should also cultivate the virtue. In this case that means we should embrace the Leaven of the Kingdom.[101] Receiving Kingdom leaven means that the values, power, and grace of heaven are manifest here and now in and through our lives.

The pattern of the world is like the Old Testament Law. When something unclean touched something holy, it made the holy thing unclean. In the Kingdom, when the King touches something unclean, it is redeemed. We should be like that. Kingdom leaven manifest through our lives should spark healing, forgiveness, and freedom.

---

[101] Matthew 13:33

Chapter Seven
Three Resources

The Book
The Cross
The Prayers

The Book

What can we know of God, His character, and His Kingdom? What are the implications for the mission of the church? Are we just left to guess or grope in the dark? Or can we have confidence that we can come to know Him, and with study, effort, and inquiry, come to know a great deal of His will for the church?

An Ordered Universe

You walk into a dark room. Your hand glides along the wall until you find the light switch and you flip it on. If the lights don't come on, you ask, "Why?" Most of us look at the ceiling in disbelief and then flip the switch two or three more times. Did you ever wonder why we keep trying?

Your telephone rings. Barring extreme anti-social behavior or pre-occupation with other crises—like nuclear war, for example—you reach to answer the phone. If there is no voice there, you are always surprised. You just know that the phone doesn't ring unless someone has dialed our number—even if it was a mistake.

On Christmas morning, you receive a package. Inside the wrapping is a box with a red push-button on it. Most of us will push the button impulsively, and a few will wonder what the button does before they push it deliberately. It's funny, though, almost everyone does push it. Virtually no one considers the possibility that nothing will happen. No one considers the possibility that there is a button that serves no purpose. That's not the way the universe works.

Why? It's because we live in an ordered universe. We live in a world where gravity works Monday through Friday and weekends, as well. E always equals MC^2, and kittens become cats, never chrysanthemums. Sometimes the order of things is congenial—friendly to us, other times hostile, but we expect order. Even in tragic inexplicable circumstances, we ask, "Why?" and expect to find answers. Though "we see through a glass darkly"[102] we expect to be able to find answers all the time. It is frustrating when they don't come, but we don't seem to stop asking and looking for meaning.

For some reason, though, when we talk about God, it is easy to fall prey to what is, in fact, a logical *non sequitur*. Many people assume that because we do not know everything about God, that we cannot know anything—or much of anything about Him with certainty. But, people left to their own devices try to decide the length and breadth of truth. The increasingly popular position is that there is no outside rule by which truth is determined, only what the individual decides. But *that* is not truth and it is not the universe that God has created. Credited with its formation or not, He made an ordered universe that is filled with structural principles that hold it together. Abundant living rises out of obedience to Him and to the principles He has established, tragedy rises out of rebellion. The history of Israel demonstrates what happens when people become their own authority and disobey God. We have the capacity to do the same thing—to trip and fall, but we also have the capacity to be faithful. Sadly, it is rare indeed for people to choose

---

[102] I Corinthians 13:12 RSV

faithfulness as a result of insight. Faithfulness usually comes in the aftermath of disaster.

My grandfather often used to tell me, "There are three ways to learn something. Precept, example, and horrible example." I have often had to sigh and chuckle at myself for failing to respond to the precepts of the kingdom, missing the lessons from examples that are presented, and instead letting things slide until disasters teach their lesson. It's amazing how a painful lesson can motivate us to faithfulness. If the lesson is not really painful, we quickly revert to our old ways.

Years ago, when I first started flying, I remember being so confident that I could handle any situation, I decided to fly up the Snake River canyon in Texas. It was easy to ignore the warnings I had heard from more seasoned pilots about the dangers of canyon flying for the chance of an adventure and some new scenery. After a while, I began to be even more lulled by the apparent ease with which I was able to fly up the river and study the interesting rock and erosion patterns made by centuries of rushing river water. While fascinated by one particularly unusual formation, my attention was diverted too long. I felt like my heart stopped with terror as I looked ahead straight into the orange globes that warned of a high-tension power line right in my path. It drooped too low to fly under, and I was too close to fly over it. Faced with no choice other than 48,000 volts frying me and the plane, I jammed the power to max and yanked back on the control yoke. It wasn't enough, and I felt the sinking realization I was not going to clear it. At the last moment, for some reason still unknown to me except for the grace of God, I reached down and yanked the lever that extended the wing flaps. The plane shuddered and either it or I let off an audible groan. With the engine roaring, and the plane staggering like a drunk in a climb, I saw the electrical cables slip just inches under the plane. The flaps had given just enough additional lift to the wings. Needless to say, in the weeks that followed, I was *very* well behaved when I flew. But that one lesson, as painful as it was, was not enough to keep me cautious and diligent for the rest of my life. This very nearly fell into my Grandfather's third category of horrible example, but eventually even it faded from memory.

Despite the fact that we have something of a legacy of rebellion, there is a more powerful statement in the fact that faith has survived even though some generations were filled with ineptitude, independence, and even sin! The church has faithfully brought the gospel of Christ to this generation. That is a tribute to God's staying power. Besides the ongoing work of the Holy Spirit to accomplish this, the greatest tool we have is the Bible. It is the record of God working in us. It is the history of redemption. It is the revelation of God's character and plan for our lives and for human history, and for our destiny.

Time will tell what our stewardship of that gift will be. Good stewardship will mean that we have responded faithfully to what He has given us. To be found faithful will mean that we obey His call on our lives both in direction and methods. The images of the kingdom give us a broad outline of how we are to live and what we are supposed to be doing. Specific guidance rises out of the circumstances of our lives and the application of what He has shown us.

Of God's many revelations, the Bible is particularly helpful in establishing a theology of what He is like. It also gives us insight into what we are called to do and be. Consistently in the written word, He demonstrates that His character is creative, loving, and redemptive. Always, He reaches beyond Himself to include others who are outside His love. Marvelously, this is not at the exclusion of those who know Him already, but instead the community and the fellowship is enriched as He reaches out. The same thing holds true for us as we reach out.

In the opening verses of his gospel, John declares the outreach of God and His limitlessness, proclaiming, "The Word became flesh and dwelt among us, full of grace and truth."[103] With that simple statement, God breaks into human history as God and man. Jesus reveals two natures; one human and one divine in one Person. We do not speak of Jesus as a Godly man, rather, we say, "God is like Jesus." Is God loving? Look at Jesus loving. Does God heal? Look at Jesus healing. Does God forgive? Listen to the words of forgiveness that Jesus speaks. In everything He does, He shows that His character is creative and loving. Jesus is ministering to the world on behalf of the Father. It is a ministry of reconciliation and outreach, seeking to reach out to those outside Himself. He refuses to be content with His own blessedness, but chooses instead to give up security to risk sharing himself.

The Word of God is a person. He became flesh and dwelt among us. There is also a written record of His coming and His character. It is the Bible. Rather than being like other books, the Bible is filled with inspiration. Inspiration (literally "in-spiriting") is found in the events themselves, and the place and timing of them. The inspiration also extends to writing the texts and the preservation of the documents over centuries of time. Though there were many people involved in the writing, the most important One involved is God. There are a number of attributes of God. One of them is that He reveals Himself and the truths of the Kingdom. Rather than being like manmade religions where teaching is put together to attempt to describe the universe and human existence, Biblical faith relies on revelation. The revelation in Scripture is utterly reliable.

A good deal of energy has been invested through the centuries in trying to discern and describe exactly *how* the Bible is inspired. Did God dictate the words to the authors so they acted just like scribes

---

[103] John 1:14

129

taking dictation? This theory is called "verbal inspiration." But the Bible describes itself and though there are places where God says, "Write this down," it does not claim that it all came to be in that way. Others think that God inspired people to write things using their personalities. Some are confused, but they can't really say if God's influence fades and man's kicks in.

Added to the complications of the situation is the fact that different parts of the Bible are written differently. Parts of the Bible are clearly historical. Some are poetic. Some are written metaphorically and some allegorically. Some are prophetic and some apocalyptic. Different parts are presented differently. It just can't be read mechanically if we are to apply it faithfully. For example, when Jesus says, "I am the door," we don't ask, "Is He oak or pine?" We are to feast on the scriptures and learn from them, but we can do so with utter confidence. There are two preeminent principles.

The first one is that whatever the style of the writing, whether allegorical, poetic, or whatever, the correct reading of a scripture passage can never be at odds with the plain sense of the text. In other words, when Jesus says, "I am the way, the truth, and the life," it is simply *not* legitimate to say that what He *really* means is that "He is *not* the way, the truth and the life."

The second principle is that the Biblical text that is delivered to us is *exactly* what God wanted us to have and *exactly* what we need. In other words, it is *utterly* reliable. To say anything less is to do violence to Who God has said and revealed that He is. If He is not powerful enough to shape the Bible through *some* means to get it to be what it needs to be for our benefit, then He is not worth following, much less worshipping.

Plainly put, the Bible should be read *naturally*, treating it historically when it presents itself as historical, poetically when it presents poetry, etc. It has stood the test of time and has never been proven wrong. For it to be less than totally reliable is completely inconsistent with the character of God. It is also utterly incompatible with the way Jesus treated the text. He demonstrated complete confidence in it. That alone should be good enough for us.

God's inspiration also extended to the compilation of which writings to include and which to leave out. And then there is the inspiration that comes to us as the Holy Spirit quickens passages for our understanding in a new way.

The Bible is, however, a complicated book (or library). For example, in one place it teaches us to confront those who have sinned against us. In another, we are told to overlook offense for love's sake. To find the truth of which principle should be applied in a given situation, we need to have help from the Holy Spirit. We should read the Bible as though the words were written on pages of glass through which we look into the face of Jesus. He is the one who will direct our lives by the power of the Holy Spirit. In time, we can come to see with the eyes of Jesus and even come to know the mind of Christ. Until then, we can just ask Him.

I was sitting with Archbishop Jonathan Onyemelukwe in the chapel he had built in his home in Onitsha, Nigeria. We were talking about the Kingdom and the voice of God. He said, "When the British came to this region with the Gospel, we met Jesus Christ as Lord. Now we don't have to go to England or ask the British what Jesus wants us to do, we can ask Him for ourselves." People who have met Jesus, can do the same thing. We don't have to wonder if it will work, either.

> If any of you lacks wisdom, let him ask of God, who gives to all liberally and without reproach, and it will be given to him. 6 But let him ask in faith, with no doubting, for he who doubts is like a wave of the sea driven and tossed by the wind. 7 For let not that man suppose that

131

he will receive anything from the Lord; <u>8</u> *he is* a double-minded man, unstable in all his ways.[104]

When we read scripture and make it part of our lives, there are huge benefits. Look at what David wrote:

> How can a young man cleanse his way?
> By taking heed according to Your word.
> With my whole heart I have sought You;
> Oh, let me not wander from Your commandments!
> Your word I have hidden in my heart,
> That I might not sin against You.[105]

The revolution in this is that the Bible does not just offer information, it offers transformational *power*. This is a reflection of a broader Kingdom value. God has chosen to manifest His power through His Word. When He created, He *spoke* everything into being. He spoke His word through prophets. When the time was full for redemption, the Word became flesh.

If we are wise, we will learn from this: there is power in the spoken word. Both creatively and destructively.

I was in a grocery store one time while wearing a clerical collar. There was a woman in the store with her young son. She was obviously having a frazzled day. Her frustration kept rising as he hopped and twirled in classic three year old fashion. When he knocked over one of those pyramids of cereal boxes, she just lost it.

"I can't believe you," she cried. "You are such a klutz. You are so uncoordinated you will never amount to anything." By this time, she was pretty well out of control and, seeing my collar, pointed at

---

[104] James 1:5-8
[105] Psalm 119:8-11

me and exclaimed, "…and if you don't straighten up I'll take you to that man and he'll have **GOD GET YOU!**".

For a second I was stunned, but then decided I had to say something. I went over to the boy and knelt down so I was closer to his height. I gave him a hug and said, "Don't worry, God loves you just like you are. Your mommy's just having a bad day."

Then I gave one of my cards to the woman and told her, "You just can't do that. You're obviously having a bad day, but your words are wounding your son. Call my office, I'll arrange for you to get some counseling so you can cope more appropriately."

She burst into tears and said, "I don't know what's gotten into me! Even though my life's out of control, I didn't mean that. I guess I really need some help."

While that was a particularly dramatic example, most of us can remember times when words have been spoken over us that have the power of curses.

How much more redemptive it is for us to speak scriptural truth over people and into circumstances that surround us. We have the power to speak life into other people's lives.

The Cross—The Power and Glory
The Cross of Jesus Christ is nothing short of a revolution. Rather than just being an event in time, The Cross is really a series of events that stand outside time. When theologians speak of "The Cross," they don't just mean the time period when Jesus was nailed to its wood. They mean the passion, suffering, death, and resurrection of Christ. One of the component parts of that cannot be separated from the others. Each one is a critical part of the other.

The Cross provides us not only the means of salvation, but also a window into God's heart. Liberal modern theologians who don't understand redemption try to steer away from The Cross, because they see it as tragically unnecessary. Some have even described it as an egregious example of child abuse. George Bernard Shaw wrote about this saying:

> The Order of Common Prayer is saturated with the ancient and to me quite infernal superstition of atonement by blood sacrifice, which I believe Christianity must get rid of if it is to survive among thoughtful people. Neither the Carthaginians nor the Mexicans ever, so far as I know, gave as a reason (to propitiate their deity) that "God so loved the world" that he had to be propitiated in this horrible way.[106]

Even though that looks like something out of the liberal playbook, nothing could be further from the truth. Those who ask, "what kind of God would send His own Son to a horrible death?" are forgetting the doctrine of the Trinity that reveals the heart of the Father was crucified along with the body of Jesus. The Father did not sentence His Son to die for others; God the Father, God the Son, and God the Holy Spirit in their essential unity decided that it was the only way to deal with sin. Because God exists outside of time, the past, present, and future all exist to him just as the present does to us. No matter how small and long ago, any sin I have committed exists forever in front of the Father. Because He is both eternal and omnipresent, my sin will ever be there no matter where I go. We needed a solution to actually deal with sin or we would forever stay under its curse. The Cross provides exactly that; a way for our sins to disappear into the death of Jesus. In His magnificent

---

[106] G.B. Shaw, "Denouncing the Book of Common Prayer," *St. Martin's Review* 33.2 (March 31, 1940)

sacrifice, Jesus offers a solution to the burden of our sin. In the resurrection, He provides a mechanism to be victorious over its power.

The Cross redefines the extravagance of the Father's heart. It redefines giving, loving, and sin. The Cross is like a lens through which we look to see what the Father and the Kingdom of Heaven are really like. It also provides a lens for God to look at us and see us without sin. God's "Cross vision" sees us as being without "spot or blemish" even when we still have a long way to go to catch up with that vision.

As I write this particular bit, I am traveling en-route between London's two airports, Heathrow and Gatwick. It is one of the least convenient flight connection arrangements, but usually not overwhelming. The trip between the airports is about forty miles, and can be pretty dreary, especially when traffic backs up on the M-25 "Motorway" that circles the city. I wrote in a journal: "Today posed particular challenges because it had been raining and BBC Radio said there had been a massive pile-up. It would have been quite depressing to crawl along at 10 mph with dark stormy sky, but I was encouraged by one of the brightest rainbows I have ever seen. The colors were brilliant against the nearly black rain clouds that were heavily laden with rain. We moved so slowly the rainbow seemed to hang there forever reinterpreting the dark sky. Brilliant and transparent, it was a victorious statement over the storm and the traffic. Looking through it into the storm clouds, into a patch of clear blue sky was a dramatic image; a signpost to another victory in another storm."

The Cross is like that rainbow, a Prism that stands against the dark suffering of Jesus, separating the bright white light of the Kingdom making a whole range of colorful truths about the Kingdom of God. It is like a lens to help all the key principles of the Kingdom come into focus.

135

The standard colors in the visible light spectrum of the rainbow are red, orange, yellow, green, blue, indigo, and violet. (ROYGBIV) Each one is a reminder of something that is radically and forever changed by the Cross.

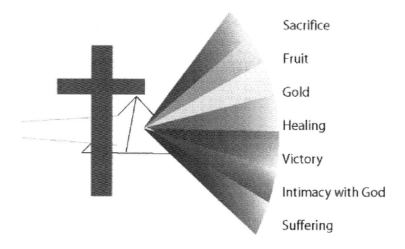

Sacrifice

Fruit

Gold

Healing

Victory

Intimacy with God

Suffering

Let's call **red** the color of sacrifice. After all, the life is in the blood; all life belongs to God (He called it forth) and blood has been the currency of sacrifice since the Fall. But the sacrifices of the Old Testament of turtledoves, lambs, and bulls are overwhelmed by the sacrifice on the Cross.

> For the law, having a shadow of the good things to come, *and* not the very image of the things, can never with these same sacrifices, which they offer continually year by year, make those who approach perfect. 2 For then would they not have ceased to be offered? For the worshipers, once purified, would have had no more consciousness of sins. 3 But in those *sacrifices there is* a reminder of sins

every year. <u>4</u> For *it is* not possible that the blood of bulls and goats could take away sins.[107]

So, God comes to the Cross. He has prefigured what is about to happen by designing an elaborate system of sacrifices. They are all designed to show that death is in sin. The blood from the sacrifices is a symbol of life being poured into death. That is what happens in earnest in the Cross of Christ. His life is poured into our death and His life overwhelms death. The Cross, however, is not just the punctuation of a series of other sacrifices. It's not just that it was the last one that was necessary. It is infinitely, creatively, and tragically greater. It is the creator offering Himself on behalf of every created one and the created order, as well. It is not just another sacrifice, it is the great-granddaddy of all sacrifices. It is unspeakably, infinitely, and magnificently more costly than any other sacrifice that has ever been contemplated, planned, or offered. If all the bulls, goats, and doves already offered were a single grain of sand, The Cross is the whole shore—the whole planet—it is everything. And what can be accomplished by this extravagant sacrifice? Everything. Nothing less.

Before The Cross, there was no escape from the problem that sin separates us from God. It is not because He stops loving us, but because we are wounded in the place where intimacy with God is supposed to take place. To add insult to injury, because God is eternal and exists outside time, any sin, no matter how small and no matter how long ago, is before the Father as real to Him today as tough it is being committed in the present time. Without the mechanism of The Cross and the death of Christ, there is nowhere else for sin to go. It still stays there labeling us, mocking, and shaming us. But The Cross changes all that. Now, in the words of

---

[107] Hebrews 10:1-4

an old Nancy Honeytree song, "clean before my Lord I stand, and in me not one blemish does He see."[108]

The sacrifice of the Cross redefines the whole sacrificial system. It gives new weight to glory and new meaning to costliness. While many people express revulsion at the horror of the Cross, there is another invasive edge to it. Such sacrifice on the part of God demands an appropriate response from us. Only now, it is no longer appropriate to speak of how much *we* sacrifice. We have been outdone. We have been gifted with a sacrifice on our behalf so costly it can never be repaid, no matter how lavishly we try. We can't even make a dent in the process. The best we can do is to honor God by respecting the value of what he has given for us and responding with our devotion. Rich or poor, the cost of the sacrifice of allegiance we are to offer is the same for each of us.

God offers Himself as a sacrifice without limit and overwhelms the elaborate system of Levitical sacrifices. No longer does He ask for small sacrifices for small offenses and large ones for the sin of nations. What He asks is simple, but desperately difficult. He asks us to give ourselves to Him. Jesus, from the Cross, cries out, "Come follow me!" What He asks from us in return is simple; simply *everything*.

I still remember hearing Argentine pastor Juan Carlos Ortiz preach in London about the pearl of great price. When Jesus challenges a man to give everything, the man replies, "If I give you all my money, how will I put gas in my car?"

Jesus replies, "You have a car? If you give all to me, the car comes, too."

---

[108] Nancy Honeytree, *Clean before my Lord, Honeytree-The First Album* (Myrrh, 1973).

"But if I give you my car, how will I get home?"

"You have a home? You say you give me all, give your home to me."

"If I give you my home, where will my family live?"

"You have a family?"

Yes, it's true. Houses, cars, bank accounts, family, sins, failures, hopes, and dreams—He wants them all.

The next color in the spectrum is **orange**. Like the citrus that bears it's name, it reminds us of the Fruit of the Spirit. St. Paul describes the fruit of living in the Spirit:

> But the fruit of the Spirit is love, joy, peace, longsuffering, kindness, goodness, faithfulness, gentleness, self-control.[109]

People may think that they are pursuing new jobs, money, status or things, but the real goal of the pursuit of those things is the fruit of the Spirit. What difference does it make if we get that new job, car, suit, toy, or spouse if it doesn't bring the fruit we desired? In today's relatively thoughtless culture, people may think that their life will be fulfilled by the object, position, or status they pursue, but what they really want is the internal fruit that they think it will produce. When I was in High School, every male-child in the place wanted the same thing: a 1956 Chevy with a Hurst shifter, Lear 8-track tape player, and fuzzy dice on the rear view mirror. But it wasn't *really* the car we wanted, though that's what we thought. We really wanted the things that the car would bring: transportation, power, status, and girls! Those things, too, were

---

[109] Galatians 5:22-23

means to an internal end. What we really wanted was love, joy, and peace.

When I was a pilot in the US Air Force, I was very deliberate in the pursuit of a very specific lifestyle. I was absolutely convinced if I could get XYZ and do ABC I would be satisfied inside. Only something went terribly wrong. One morning I woke up and realized that I had hit each of the marks I had set. It wasn't that I had acquired everything I imagined I wanted, but I had done enough and gotten enough to know that I was on the right track of my plan. I had essentially realized the life I had imagined would bring me such joy and peace but it didn't. In fact, I fell so horribly short I knew that I was completely on the wrong track. As I realized that I had absolutely no idea what would fill the sense of emptiness in my life, I lay in bed and my eyes filled up with tears, making tiny pools over my eyes. It was devastating. It wasn't frustration of not being able to meet the bar I had set, it was devastation at hitting the bar and not having it make a difference.

It wasn't stuff, position, power, travel, or money. It wasn't having a great job flying jets. It wasn't even having friends who saw me fly across the Pacific Ocean one week and to Europe the next. It wasn't accumulating beautiful things and getting satisfaction from them. What was so utterly devastating was realizing I didn't know what to do to find "inner peace." There I was in a crisis of realizing and despairing. I didn't know what I should be doing instead of what I had been doing. As I lay in bed something came crashing into my memory. Someone had once said to me, "In every man there is a God-shaped void that only Jesus Christ can fill. Remember that, it's going to be important in your life."

Thinking about that was both exciting and horrific. Being a follower of Jesus had always seemed to me to be too expensive. I thought of it as giving things up. Now for the first time it occurred to me that inner fulfillment could come not from what I *had* but

140

who I was. One of the first heartfelt prayers I ever prayed was, "Lord, you can even make me weird if you make me happy." It was not long after that Jesus quickened my heart and spirit.

As my relationship with the Lord began to come alive, I noticed something else. The peace I had been seeking began to appear. The more I tried to conform my life to what He said, the better things got. It wasn't really a matter of sacrificing for Him. It was really *investing* in the Kingdom.

Years ago, I heard a lady ask a Bible teacher named Terry Fullam, "Where does the fruit of the Spirit come from?"

Without even pausing he said, "The fruit of the Spirit is grown in the garden of obedience."

Then he took a breath. "My," he said, "that's good. It's so good in fact, I know I'm not that smart. That answer, Madam, came from the Lord!"

On the Cross, we see Jesus being obedient. The fruit of His obedience is the salvation of the world. As the Cross stands, it challenges us to a higher standard of obedience than we could ever have imagined. It also promises us a much richer harvest of fruit for our internal lives than we could ever have otherwise. The Holy Spirit calls fruit to life in us that is far more abundant than we have a right to expect. The idea is that we will make the fruit available to the world around us that is starving for what the Holy Spirit provides.

The Kingdom and Wealth

The next color on the spectrum is **yellow** (or gold). Yellow is a reminder that the Cross changes everything about money, wealth, and possessions. Just as the fruit of the Spirit is revolutionized by Jesus' death, money is, too.

The Old Testament taught the pattern of tithing. That meant ten percent to the Lord through the church (storehouse). Now there is a new standard. God doesn't ask for ten percent anymore. He asks for *everything*. It's not that He gets 10% and I get 90. The Cross cries out, "How could you ever repay love like this?" The Cross magnifies the principle of stewardship to challenge us to respond to magnificent love. The Cross is there, not only at the offering plate and mission fundraiser. It is also there towering over every purchase and every expenditure. It is even present in the marketplace in every business transaction. Sadly, many miss its presence and impact. Even though it is imposing, it can still be ignored.

Not long after I had come into a relationship with the Lord, I decided to have a big formal ceremony giving everything I had to Jesus. I went around my apartment putting my hand on things and saying, "This is yours now, Lord." I prayed over my car and even my checkbook. A few days later, without a prayer or a thought, I saw a new twelve-string guitar and *had* to have it. I bought it on the spot. Even as I walked out of the store, I was uncomfortable. It was so awkward I didn't even want to take it home. I wound up leaving it at a friend's house before I ever took it to mine.

Suddenly, I realized what I had done. I had *said* everything belonged to the Lord but then didn't even ask if buying the guitar was part of His plan. I wonder if I didn't ask because I didn't want to run the risk of having Him say, "No."

Convicted, I told Him, "I'll return it, Lord, or give it away."

"Not necessary," came the reply. I just want you to remember *Whose* it is."

In some circles, poverty is espoused as a virtue. Jesus Himself was quite clear that "The poor you will always have with you."[110] In that, He is *not* saying that poverty is to be celebrated, He was saying that it is an inevitable result of this sinful and fallen world. He also encourages us to do something about it. When we understand that money and possessions are not *ours*, but are given into our hands as stewards, riches can come; but, rightly used, they benefit the Kingdom rather than just expanding our lifestyle. Solomon makes it clear in Proverbs that righteousness produces riches, but the riches of the Kingdom are not necessarily the same thing as riches in the world.

> Treasures of wickedness profit nothing,
> But righteousness delivers from death.
> The LORD will not allow the righteous soul to famish,
> But He casts away the desire of the wicked.
> He who has a slack hand becomes poor,
> But the hand of the diligent makes rich.[111]

Righteous living will produce abundant fruit. It is important to remember, however, that the fruit that the Kingdom will produce is Kingdom fruit, not necessarily money. It is really disconcerting to realize that money can do a lot of harm, as well as good. It can certainly make it much easier to indulge the flesh. On the Kingdom side, though, when material wealth comes, it brings resources that are intended to bear Kingdom fruit. In the light of the Cross, the Kingdom principle of "sowing and reaping" is manifest expressly so the work of the Kingdom is equipped to have "an abundance for every good work." People who give will, in fact, "get," but righteousness calls us to a different pattern than just giving to get. In the Kingdom, the principle is: *Give, receive, in order to give more to equip every good work.*

---

[110] Matthew 26:11
[111] Proverbs 10:2-4

But this *I say:* He who sows sparingly will also reap sparingly, and he who sows bountifully will also reap bountifully. <u>7</u> *So let* each one *give* as he purposes in his heart, not grudgingly or of necessity; for God loves a cheerful giver. <u>8</u> And God *is* able to make all grace abound toward you, that you, always having all sufficiency in all *things,* may have an abundance for every good work. <u>9</u> As it is written:

> *He has dispersed abroad,*
> *He has given to the poor;*
> *His righteousness endures forever.* "[112]

There is much more to say about Kingdom economics, but for now, suffice it to say that things eternal will always have greater glory than things temporal. When God comes to the Cross and pours out all that He is, how things are valued is changed forever. Before the Cross, people might argue that a person's worth is determined by what they have done, or what they might do to add value to the world. Now we find our true value from what Someone else is willing to pay. Suddenly, you are worth the life of God. The world has been very wrong for a very long time about what things are worth and what the priorities of resources and economics are. It assumes that material wealth brings joy and satisfaction. Instead, God Himself has modeled that it is the eternal that brings satisfaction. Like the Lord who has given us life, Kingdom dwellers are givers. Never looking for the least that can be given, we should love to be extravagant in what we give.

Nurture, Health, and Healing-Green
Though it may be a huge disappointment to agnostics, the universe is not random. It is laid out with purpose and order. Living things

---

[112] 1 Corinthians 9:6-9

grow and reproduce. Because we are in a fallen world, sometimes there is sickness, bondage, and even death. It is crucial to understand, however, that God is never the source of sickness. God is good. If there is sickness, lack, or death it has not come from Him. It is the devil who comes to "steal, kill, and destroy."[113]

When we become people of the Cross (and people of the Kingdom), the realities of the Kingdom should become our passions and purpose. Think of the words of the Lord's prayer: "Thy Kingdom come, Thy will be done on earth as it is in heaven..."

We are supposed to look to heaven as the pattern for our lives and ministries. Are there sick people in Heaven? Are there broken relationships in Heaven? Are there addictions in Heaven? Is anyone in prison there?

If we pray for the earth to become like the Kingdom of Heaven, we should yearn, long, and strive for the Kingdom to be manifest here on earth. Power for transformation rises from the Cross as it does from the Resurrection. They are part of the same process. Even though there may be times when we pray and don't see healing come quickly (or in any way that we expect), our vocation is to pray for the Kingdom to come. Because of the Cross, we can do so with confidence. The more we pray, the more we will see fruit. The more we pray, the more we will understand.

Works of Power and Manifest Victory-Blue

At the time, no one realized it, but the Cross was the greatest manifestation of Power ever released. It was/is the focal point of God reversing sin's corruption, stealing its power, and the place where death is forever humiliated. It was absolute and total victory, but rather than bursting into the world in a huge, bright electrical

---

[113] John 10:10

145

shock, it looked like a whimpering, humiliating defeat. Once again, to see another of the great principles of the Kingdom one must look beyond the obvious way things appear. A missed plane, a lost job, the death of the Savior all look to be defeat incarnate, but our vision is limited and we don't *know*. There is a great element of trust required to stay peaceful in the midst of circumstances that look in every way to be adverse. There is no doubt that they can be painful, but aren't always. The circumstances that have escaped our notice or knowledge would, if known, show that they are helpful, even friendly to us. Not until we have the whole picture can we understand. Even then, understanding is not our job. The great sin of the Garden was deciding for themselves what was good and what was evil. That's what they were after in feasting on the fruit of the knowledge of good and evil. It's not that God doesn't want us to know good from bad, He just doesn't want us deciding for ourselves which is which. He is the One who knows. He is the One who decides. We are the ones who are supposed to obey.

Here is a powerful lesson from the Cross. Great victories can rise from great pain. It may seem that all is lost, but it is not so to God. That is what the Cross demonstrates. The issue for us is *trust*. When we commend our lives and our future to God, doesn't it make sense to believe that He can be trusted with it?

What, though, does Kingdom victory look like? The thing is, we don't know. We simply don't have enough information—at least we don't at the start of our journey. The only way to define spiritual victory with any measure of confidence is *obedience*. Obedience produces fruit. Obedience brings life. Obedience produces victory.

Intimacy with God-Indigo

In the Temple, a great and elaborate system of curtains hung to block the view and the way to the Holy of Holies. It even overlapped at the middle so it wouldn't accidentally allow access. In fact, it was the High Priest alone, and then only on the Day of Atonement that anyone even entered the Holy place.

> **1** "Moreover you shall make the tabernacle *with* ten curtains *of* fine woven linen and blue, purple, and scarlet *thread;* with artistic designs of cherubim you shall weave them. **2** The length of each curtain *shall be* twenty-eight cubits, and the width of each curtain four cubits. And every one of the curtains shall have the same measurements. **3** Five curtains shall be coupled to one another, and *the other* five curtains *shall be* coupled to one another.[114]

As Jesus cried "It is finished" from the Cross, the veil of the curtain was torn from top to bottom. Of course, it symbolized God's anguish, but the main thing it demonstrated was that access to the throne room was forever granted. Even more magnificently, what is figured in the rent veil of the Temple is manifest in our lives, as intimacy with God is reestablished and His Spirit comes to dwell in us. This is a return to the garden, but even more than just turning back the clock. It is restoration full of the knowledge of the pain and consequences of sin. Even better than the glory that the angels know, our redemption sees the reversal of sin, the restoration of our relationship with God, and the healing of our identity. Now, we can become who we were created to be.

Intimacy with God produces a "secret place" where we meet with Him for worship and for transformation. What happens there will carry us though difficult times.

> For in the time of trouble
> He shall hide me in His pavilion;

---

[114]Exodus 26:1-3

In the secret place of His tabernacle
He shall hide me;
He shall set me high upon a rock.
6 And now my head shall be lifted up above my enemies all
around me;
Therefore I will offer sacrifices of joy in His tabernacle; I will
sing, yes, I will sing praises to the LORD.[115]

Suffering and Commitment-Violet/Purple

Call me crazy, but I like parties and gifts more than getting
attacked and beaten up. Maybe it's just me, but I have always
found presents and affirmations more enjoyable than wounds and
insults. But the truth is that the most fruitful things that have come
from my life have not been the fun things—they have come from
the costly things.

I heard a preacher once say, "My grandfather used to say, 'When
I'm faced with a choice about life in the Kingdom, I ask the
question, 'What's the most costly option?' That's the one that's
likely to be closest to the heart of God.'" I've thought about that
many times and have tried to find a way to disagree, but the truth
is, that's the way the Kingdom works. Suffering can produce glory!

> Therefore we do not lose heart. Even though our
> outward man is perishing, yet the inward *man* is being
> renewed day by day. 17 For our light affliction, which is
> but for a moment, is working for us a far more exceeding
> *and* eternal weight of glory...[116]

When we look at the suffering that Jesus undertook on the Cross
for our benefit, we see a deeper love and a cost more dear than has
ever been manifest before or ever will be. If we will dare to look on

---

[115] Psalm 27:5-6
[116] 2 Corinthians 4:16-17

the suffering of Jesus and contemplate both the wounds and the love poured out there, it will certainly call us to a higher standard of service, suffering, and love; and we can press on in confidence.

> Seeing then that we have a great High Priest who has passed through the heavens, Jesus the Son of God, let us hold fast *our* confession. 15 For we do not have a High Priest who cannot sympathize with our weaknesses, but was in all *points* tempted as *we are, yet* without sin. 16 Let us therefore come boldly to the throne of grace, that we may obtain mercy and find grace to help in time of need.[117]

---

[117] Hebrews 4:14-16

Section 2

Chapter Eight
Three Aspects of the Father

The Lord's Prayer

While The Cross provides us with a lens for Kingdom sight, the Lord's Prayer provides us with a pattern of Kingdom living. We can find out Who He is, who we are, and something of how we are to live.

Our Father...
There is a King
Who He is.

While I was doing doctoral research in the 1980's, I heard about a church of over six hundred thousand members. More remarkably, they were organized into small home groups of ten or fifteen people. I decided to go to Seoul, Korea to learn from the man who had led the remarkable growth. In Korea, they call him Cho Yongi, but in Western terms his name is Paul Yongi Cho (more recently he is called David). I attended seminars and lectures, and even had the opportunity on several occasions to sit in his office. He is a remarkable and humble man who clearly sees that it is God who has done the work. Pastor Cho says his job is to pray and get out of the way.

It is a huge complex with a main sanctuary that seats about thirty thousand people, and a dozen or so other auditoriums that seat around a thousand tucked away around the campus. Other meetings are linked by video and meet in other locations around the city. During the week, at virtually every hour of every day, small groups meet in homes led by ordinary Christian leaders. To gather the home group leaders, they hire the Olympic stadium. It seats 118,000 and they fill it up.

One Friday when I was up in the office, the church had a leaders' meeting scheduled for the next day at 4:00 pm. The plan was to gather early enough so that people could still travel to their families to participate in Independence Day celebrations the day after the meeting. One of the administrative assistants came in and said that a message had come in from the government. A military practice had been scheduled for the Independence Day parade that would close the main road leading to the stadium. It would no longer be possible to have the meeting at 4:00 pm. Unphased, Pastor Cho simply said, "No problem, move the leaders' meeting to two o'clock."

I was utterly dumbfounded. With month's of preparation my church had trouble getting people to show up at the right time when daylight savings changed. He had just directed a change for nearly 120,000 people for the next day!

I had been invited to be down on the playing field of the stadium for the meeting. At two o'clock sharp, I looked around the stadium and saw a sea of people who had been contacted through magnificent lines of communication and authority. They had been given the new time and had shown up.

A few days later I asked how they had managed to do it. In fact, we were talking about the whole process. The answer was simple: infrastructure and prayer. Another Korean pastor who was also visiting asked, "How is it that my church has 3,000 people and yours has over 600,000?"

Pastor Cho answered, "How much do you pray?"

The answer came, "About two hours a day." (I was impressed.)

Cho said, "I pray eight. Maybe that's part of it."

My mind was racing and I couldn't stop considering, "How does a person pray for eight hours?" In fact, how do people pray for an hour?

The answer is surprisingly simple. It does not take superhuman effort. I went to Korea wondering how anyone could pray for several hours a day and saw the powerful transferable way that prayer is taught. I came home doing it. While others have doubtless done similar things through the centuries, the pattern that Pastor Cho teaches is to use the Lord's Prayer as a pattern for prayer and to pray through it. Experience the love of Abba Father, pray through His "holy" names, then pray and long for the Kingdom to be established, and so on. It is a magnificent template and encouragement.

Our Father Who art in heaven...

In His revolutionary prayer, Jesus taught the disciples to pray, "Abba" (father).

No matter how gracious, loving, or committed our earthly fathers are, they are the most clear and dramatic icons that shape our thinking about what our Heavenly Father is like. While there are inspirational fathers on the earth, none are able to love with the sacrificial love of the Father. The term for this kind of love in Hebrew is חֶסֶד *hesed,* and has a parallel term in Greek--*agape* (αγαπη).

Because in the human sphere we have never seen utterly unconditional love, the unconscious assumption is that the love of the Father must be in some ways limited, too. I'd been converted,

155

set on fire by the Holy Spirit, and ordained, and had taught many times on the Love of God. But, I had no idea how limited my experience was.

An old church I mentioned serving had a building that would seat less than a hundred people and was built in 1727. They had a communion cup that had been made by Paul Revere and families that went *way back.* As Charles Dickens wrote, "It was the best of times and it was the worst of times." Many, many people were coming to faith, but we had dramatically out-grown the little church building. Even though I conducted multiple services on Sunday (with two of them in the historic building), the "historically rooted" people in the congregation were extremely unhappy. It would only be years later that I came to understand what was really going on. At the time, I was utterly puzzled why the "old" families in the church were so angry that many new people were coming to church and coming to life. The heart of their problem wasn't really centered on the church. It had to do with the dramatic change that their community was undergoing. I tried to pastor them, but it didn't work very well. At the heart of it, I guess I felt that people who were angry that others were meeting Jesus were just wrong, and probably bad people, though I didn't want to think or talk that way. As the tensions increased, I retreated into work to bring more and more people into the church.

Though I kept trying, I didn't understand the old-timers and their historically rooted perspective. One day, while having tea with a parishioner, I got an eye-opening example of the difference of their worldview and mine. In the course of conversation, this tiny lady, who had grown up on her family's plantation, said in a deep-Southern accent, "Everything has just gone to pot around here since we lost the war."

Knowing how the Civil War had deeply impacted the region, I tried to respond with my most sensitive pastoral tone. Even though the complexities were lost in it, with a strong desire to build bridges, it seemed helpful to adopt the language I had heard many times before. I put down my teacup and said, "Yes Ma'am. That war of 'Northern aggression' was a painful time."

With dismissive distain she replied, "I wasn't speaking of the recent unpleasantness. I meant the revolution!"

Her family had been given a land grant from King George. They were Tories who viewed the war for independence as a defeat.

While I began to better understand a little more of the situation, I still didn't know what to do about it. As the church grew, tensions became more and more unpleasant. It was a very hard place to be. Hardly a day went by without deeply painful conflict.

When I heard about a man named Brennan Manning, my wife Susan and I flew to New Orleans to see him to ask for his counsel and advice. On hearing the story of scores of people coming to faith, yet a church filled with tension and anxiety, he agreed to come. Brennan is an amazing speaker with a powerful story.

He came for a week and taught and listened. He heard stories from people and got an earful about the conflicts. On the last night he was there, as he spoke at the church, he said, "I came to experience the unconditional love of my Abba Father not because of the good I'd done, but because He is an extravagant lover."

Continuing, he slowly got down on his hands and knees on the altar steps and continued, "One morning I woke up on Commercial Boulevard in Fort Lauderdale, Florida in an alcoholic fog, covered in my own vomit. My shoes had been stolen by some wine-o during the night. I thought my head would explode. A woman was walking down the sidewalk with her young son. When he got in front of me he stopped, with that staring kind of fascination that children can have. He just stood there. His mother jerked him by the arm and said, 'Don't even look at that. That's nothing but filth,' and spit on me in disgust."

Still on his hands and knees, with the people stunned and speechless, he continued, "I have sinned more than any of you. I have plumbed deeper into the depths of sin than you can imagine and yet, I have come to know not the wrath I thought I deserved from God, but His absolute and unconditional love." With a grief that sounded like the heartbreak that the Father must have at our sin, he went on, "All that being said, I must tell you with sadness, that I have never in my life experienced a group of people who more desperately need to experience the unconditional love of God. I implore you to let Him love you."

People were weeping by this time and the service finished in silence. There was nothing that could be said.

Later, in the middle of the night, I lay in bed unable to sleep. Welling up inside me was a terrible sense of failure. I knew that by God's grace I had worked to grow the church, but I had not loved the people as I should have. It was beyond terrible. I hurt so deeply that I literally thought I would split in two. Now sobbing at my failures, I prayed through tearful gasps, "I have nothing to offer you," and felt like an utter failure. For the first time, it even seemed irrelevant that I had enjoyed evangelistic successes. I knew that I had fallen horribly short.

Though I had prayed for forgiveness of sins many times and had taught on the grace and love of God, I had not recognized His *unconditional* acceptance. Expecting to hear horrible words of condemnation from the Lord, I was startled to hear Him speak tenderly to me out loud. Though it came through the voice of my wife reaching to hold me as I wept, His words were, "You are wonderful to me. You are wonderful to me." Over and over the words repeated as I fought back and replied, "But I have nothing to offer you!"

Still the words came, "You are wonderful to me," she spoke for Him over and over until they began to sink in. Eventually, the truth of His love overwhelmed me as my sobs changed to tears of relief.

There is a huge difference between the conviction of the Holy Spirit and the condemnation that comes from the devil. While it was painful to experience the conviction of the Lord, redemption quickly followed repentance. That is what God wants us to experience. The evil one wants us to be incapacitated by shame.

> Guilt says "you did something wrong," but shame says, "you are faulty." Guilt may be a fact; shame is a feeling...If you feel shame, you are receiving the lies of the enemy instead of the grace of Christ's death on the Cross that covers your sin and shame.[118]

From that moment, my life was forever changed. In an instant, I served a new Principle. He had given what could not be taken. What was washing off of me was the false conviction that God would love me better if I served Him better. What began in a moment of time has continued for decades; not flawlessly, of course, but indelibly.

What is important is that it is for every Christian to have their own *experience* of the unconditional love of the Father. It is simply not enough to *believe* that He loves us. To be carried through life's anguishes, we need something more. Not just the aroma of the banquet, but the flavor, texture, and soporific excellence of it. And

---

[118] Terry Moore, *The Cross is the Key*. (Lewisville: Paradigm Publishing, 2006). Page 41

not just so we can endure. We need it so we can prosper in the Kingdom and *proclaim and bring transformation!* Remember the words of Isaiah:

> "The Spirit of the Lord GOD *is* upon Me,
>> Because the LORD has anointed Me
>> To preach good tidings to the poor;
> He has sent Me to heal the brokenhearted,
>> To proclaim liberty to the captives,
>> And the opening of the prison to *those who are* bound;
> To proclaim the acceptable year of the LORD,
>> And the day of vengeance of our God;
>> To comfort all who mourn,
> To console those who mourn in Zion,
>> To give them beauty for ashes,
>> The oil of joy for mourning,
>> The garment of praise for the spirit of heaviness;
>> That they may be called trees of righteousness,
>> The planting of the LORD, that He may be glorified."[119]

He has come to us to do all this and more. But He is not the only one to do this work. He calls us to carry on the work as well. Notice, as the passage continues, who it is that will rebuild old ruins and raise desolations: It is a great work that is given to us! The ones who have been set free!

> And they shall rebuild the old ruins,
> They shall raise up the former desolations,
> And they shall repair the ruined cities,
> The desolations of many generations.

---

[119] Isaiah 61:1-3

That's who we really are. Once we have actually *experienced* the love of the Father, we are changed. We are the *"they!"* We are children of God with a purpose. We are desolation healers and city re-builders. We are supposed to be fountains of hope. Our Father (Daddy) calls us to continue the work of Jesus and extend it.

> "Most assuredly, I say to you, he who believes in Me, the works that I do he will do also; and greater works than these he will do, because I go to My Father.[120]

When we drink that in, we are forever different. That experience makes everything new. But that is just the beginning of what the King wants to do as He reigns in our lives. The Father's love is the kind of love that redefines everything. Perhaps if I'd been brighter or paying closer attention, I might have caught on sooner. I might have started expecting and experiencing Kingdom living more fully sooner. But then again, I thank God that I'm opening up to it at all.

When people have lived lives of brokenness or abuse, it is hard for them to believe that God is good, but it is essential to accept it. He is thoroughly and completely good; incapable of doing bad things. There are challenges, of course, to understanding this. Sometimes He doesn't look very nice at all. Remember the Sons of Korah who were swallowed up by the earth?[121] Or what about Uzza who died when he reached out to steady the Ark?[122] And lest we think that those examples of accountability are only found in the Old Testament, we see Ananias and Sapphiria who lied about what they had given and they were struck dead.[123] The demands of holiness in the face of deception and rebellion, however, are at least

---

[120] John 14:12
[121] Numbers 16:28-35
[122] 2 Samuel 6:6
[123] Acts 5:1-4

comprehensible from a loving God in the face of assaults on His holiness.

One of the accounts that is often used to challenge the idea that God is always good is the story of the man born blind in John 9. On the surface, the text seems to support the idea that God did evil to a person with no individual culpability. Many classic translations of this passage suggest that God blinded him just so He could show off later.

> Jesus answered, "Neither this man nor his parents sinned, but that the works of God should be revealed in him. 4 I must work the works of Him who sent Me while it is day; *the* night is coming when no one can work. 5 As long as I am in the world, I am the light of the world."[124]

There is, however, a very reasonable explanation. It has to do with the translation of this passage. Remember that the Greek texts that were used from which modern translations emanate did not look like the documents we have today. In order to save valuable space on papyrus scrolls, punctuation as well as the spaces between words were omitted. It makes it a bit tricky to translate, but eventually, one can get the hang of it. The passage above, then, would look something like this:

> jesusansweredneitherthismannorhisparentssin
> nedbutthattheworksofgodshouldberevealedinh
> imimustworktheworksofhimwhosentmewhilei
> tisdaythenightiscomingwhennoonecanworkasl
> ongasiamintheworldiamthelightoftheworld

It is even more confusing and intimidating in Greek, but the principle is the same.

---

[124] John 9:3-5

απεκριθηοιησουςουτεουτοςημαρτενουτεοιγο
νειςαυτουαλλιναφανερωθηταεργατουθεουεν
αυτωεμεδειεργαζεσθαιταεργατουπεμψαντος
μεεωςημεραεστινερχεταινυξοτεουδειςδυνατα
ιεργαζεσθαιοτανεντωκοσμωωφωςειμιτουκοσ
μου

Anyway, it is just as legitimate to translate the passage slightly differently, but the result is more faithful to what God is like. By simply placing the punctuation in a different place, the meaning of the sentences are dramatically changed. Notice how it reads now with the comma between "sinned" and "but" changed to a period and the period between "him" and "I" changed to a comma:

> Jesus answered, "Neither this man nor his parents **sinned. But** that the works of God should be revealed in **him, I must** work the works of Him who sent Me while it is day; *the* night is coming when no one can work. **5** As long as I am in the world, I am the light of the world."[125]

Notice now the emphasis is now not on the man being made blind so God can show off. Now the emphasis is on the goodness of God being manifest "while it is day." In this case, "day" refers to the time Jesus (the Light of the world) was on earth. As this is the only case in the New Testament where it appears God has sent the sickness, it is an important distinction. God is good. He doesn't send or do bad things. It is the devil who comes "to steal, kill, and destroy."[126] If there is sickness or torment, it is the devil who sent it, not God. We'll talk more about God's goodness in the Kingdom later, but the point is, God only sends good our way.

---

[125] John 9:3-5
[126] John 10:9

"Every good gift and every perfect gift is from above, and comes down from the Father of lights, with whom there is no variation or shadow of turning."[127]

Hallowed be Thy Name...

When God spoke to Moses and told him to go to Pharaoh and demand the release of the Jews, Moses asked, "Who shall I say sent me?" (Exodus 3:14) God replies, "I AM that I AM." It's actually even more powerful and elegant in Hebrew. The Hebrew יהוה is rendered in English as YHWH. It is called the *tetragrammaton*. That just means "four letters," because the Jews didn't ordinarily speak the name of God. Only the High Priest would say it aloud in his prayer on the Day of Atonement. In some translations, it is rendered as "Yahweh." More than a century ago, some academic decided to merge the four letters of the tetragrammaton YHWH "pointing the text" with the vowels from the Hebrew word for Lord, *adonai*. The result was **YaHoWaH**, which became rendered in English as Jehovah.[128] YHWH or Jehovah, however, is not the only name He is called in the Bible. There are a whole series of compound modifying names He is also called.

A wonderful way to pray is to pray through the many names that God is called. They reveal wonderful things about His character. Here are a few of them. Remember that Hebrew is written from right to left. That is why the characters for YHWH יהוה appear on the right of each of these expressions.

---

[127] James 1:17
[128] This little tidbit is devastating to Jehovah's Witnesses whose main thrust is earning acceptance from God by using what they think is His *real* name: Jehovah.

YHWH M'qaddesh (The God Who Sanctifies)
יהוה קָדַשׁ

> ...we are bound to give thanks to God always for you, brethren beloved by the Lord, because God from the beginning chose you for salvation through sanctification by the Spirit and belief in the truth, <u>14</u> to which He called you by our gospel, for the obtaining of the glory of our Lord Jesus Christ.[129]

YHWH Nissi (The God of Victory, or The Lord of the Banner)
יהוה נִסִּי

Bernard Malango is from Malawi. He has pastoral oversight of more than a million Christians in four nations (Malawi, Zimbabwe, Zambia, and Botswana). If you want to track him down, it's pretty easy. Just go to the place of the deepest need, the greatest conflict, and the most thorny problem. That's where he'll most likely be. He is the first to tell you that he doesn't have all the answers. But he sees his role as an Archbishop and apostle as incarnation. Standing in the gap where the need is the greatest to remind people that God is also there, and it is under His banner that the battle is waged.

There is a link between the *banner* of the Lord and His *victory*. On the battlefield, when we see the banner, we are reminded that the Lord is there, and that He is directing the battle plan. The more serious the conflict, the more crucial it is that we get a fix on His plan. As you pray for *YHWH Nissi* to be manifest in your life, ask Him to show you how to walk and how to contend against the evil one. God has a plan and He is eager to share it with you.

One of the biggest reasons that we miss His plan is that His plan can seem ridiculous! Look at Gideon. He had a credible fighting force. God wanted it pared down to the point it was ridiculous and the only way that they could possibly prevail is with the

---

[129] 2 Thessalonians 2:13-14

miraculous intervention of God. Or, how about the plan to shout down the wall of Jericho? Not ridiculous enough? How about David setting aside armor and shield to go up against the giant!

The Lord of the Battle/Banner will prove Himself at the end of the day, but He does not want to share the spotlight with anyone or anything. He is the Holy One of Israel, and don't you ever forget it.

YHWH Jireh or Yireh (God the Provider)
יהוה יִרְאֶה

Years ago, at a point in ministry where we really didn't have any spare money (at all!), my now-married-but-then-young daughter was absolutely *crazy* for a scooter. You know the two-wheeled t-bar handle type that has a flat part to stand on while you zoom along? She was very enthusiastic and very persistent. There is no way that my wife Susan or I could have missed the point: she *wanted* a scooter. Or perhaps more accurately... she **wanted a SCOOTER!!!** It wasn't an unreasonable request, and it was pretty rare for her to get so fired up about wanting to get something, so we tried to be realistic, but encouraging.

"Let's pray for a scooter," we told her.

Every night for weeks, we prayed for God to supply a scooter. Actually, I was thinking more that He would find a way of coming up with about $100 for one. It was a good exercise for all of us, but it was *great* for her. She *knew* that God was her source and He was going to supply a scooter. I guess I wondered how high a priority it was for God for a ten year-old to get a scooter. I found out the answer. One evening when I was coming home from church, I looked at the neighbor's trash and saw a scooter, resplendent with pink streamers and girly decals sitting on top of the trash can. Except for a flat tire, it was in great shape.

The neighbor dismissed it with a wave, "It has a flat tire and she (his daughter) never rides it anyway. You're welcome to it."

I hid it in my trunk and took it to the bike shop nearby. For $1.92 they installed a new inner tube for the tire, and even polished it up. Not bad for $1.92.

The point, of course, is that God promises to supply what we need. He doesn't promise to supply everything that we *think* we need or want. He is our source. Not the company we work for or the government of our nation. He is the source and supply. It may be easier to look to other sources for what we need, but it isn't right. Pray for what you need. Ask *YHWH Jireh*.

YHWH Tsidkenu (The God of Righteousness)
יהוה צִדְקֵנוּ

The concept of righteousness comes from being straight (i.e, not bent). Think of God as being the straight-edge or the rule. It is His character that determines truth. When things are viewed next to Him, they automatically fall under judgment. "The God of Righteousness" is used as a proper name in Jeremiah.

> "Behold, *the* days are coming," says the LORD,
> "That I will raise to David a Branch of
> righteousness;
> A King shall reign and prosper,
> And execute judgment and
> righteousness in the earth.
> In His days Judah will be saved,
> And Israel will dwell safely;
> Now this *is* His name by which He will
> be called:

THE LORD OUR RIGHTEOUSNESS.[130]

Obviously, this is referring to Jesus. What is marvelous about His righteousness is that it can be transferred to us!

> For He (the Father) made (caused, *not* forced!) Him who knew no sin *to be* sin for us, that we might become the righteousness of God in Him.[131]

YHWH *Rohi* (The Lord Our Shepherd)

יהוה רָעָה

If you've ever been around sheep you know that being a shepherd is a good deal more robust than most people think. There are many challenges from things that want to assault the sheep. David spoke about his shepherding days and having to defend his wooly charges against lions, and tigers, and bears, oh my! (Well, OK, no tigers.)

I remember as a boy being caught between sheep and some sugar beets when the wind changed. As they caught a whiff of the smell (of what to sheep must be a little bit of sheepy heaven), they started running toward the sweet pile of sugar beets that had just been pulled out of the ground. I don't know exactly how many sheep there were. I was only seven, but I think there were about a million. Maybe two million. The sheep's eyes glazed over and they ran straight toward the beets in a path that would have run right over me without any concern at all (from this I figured out that sheep are not deeply concerned with human rights violations).

---

[130] Jeremiah 23:5-6
[131] 2 Corinthians 5:21

With disaster only seconds away a massive black Belgian Shepard sheepdog came zooming over following the whistles of the shepherd. With a bark or two and a handful of nips on the legs of the recalcitrant ones, I was rescued and the beets were saved. Mark two for the sheepdog.

It was wonderful to see how the sheepdog handled the situation. Good to be in such good hands…er, well, paws. Imagine how much more secure we are in the hands of the Good Shepherd. It will never be wasted energy to lay our needs and our desires at the Master's feet.

YHWH *Shalom* (The Lord is Our Peace)
יהוה שָׁלוֹם

Archbishop Benjamin Yugasuk was a beautiful man. He had coal black skin, weathered with age and a lifetime of walking everywhere, usually at night to avoid government troops. His hair was like cotton, pure white and dancing in stark contrast to his wrinkled face. His eyes were like hand-blown glass Christmas ornaments, the kind that are all shiny inside. His laughter was like a strip of those old-timey sleigh bells that they used to tack on shop doors. His tears flowed freely like diamonds, gemstones born out of heat and pressure. He was a great man and he loved me.

The first time we met, he was already old. He came to me after I had spoken about the heartbreak of the faithless liberal church in America. Glistening tears were rolling down his cheeks and he looked both tender and stricken. He held his stomach and said, "When you spoke, God grabbed me here. I will stand with you for the Gospel, no matter who comes against."

Then he reached over and took my face in his hands and pulled me down close to him and began to kiss my face as he cried. He kissed my forehead and my cheeks and then he blessed me.

169

Later, when word came that government planes were bombing his cathedral and schools in Juba, he said quietly and simply, "I have to go back and die with my people."

Benjamin ended his life, utterly used up and completely poured out. Totally spent, he had offered his life until there was nothing left but the Peace of Christ. He knew and shared the *shalom* of God. The God of Peace has promised to be with us. His peace is not the absence of conflict. It is the confidence that I am secure in Him regardless of the circumstances.

YHWH *Shammah* (The Lord Who is Present)

יהוה שָׁמָּה

> God *is* our refuge and strength,
>> A very present help in trouble.
> 2   Therefore we will not fear,
>> Even though the earth be removed,
>> And though the mountains be carried into the midst of the sea;
> 3   *Though* its waters roar *and* be troubled,
>> *Though* the mountains shake with its swelling.

Theologically, God is omnipresent. He is everywhere. But for those who acknowledge His presence, there is much more. We should encounter Him in intimacy. If He is present but ignored, what fruit is there? The point is that we spend time with Him in order to get to know Him and His ways. He will show us how and where to walk. The result is a deeper joy than the world can give.

> You will show me the path of life;
>> In Your presence *is* fullness of joy;
>> At Your right hand *are* pleasures forevermore.[132]

---

[132] Psalm 16:8

Even though the fallen world has tribulation, sin, and trouble, we can still have confidence in our relationship with Him. From His presence in our lives comes unspeakable joy.

> "These things I have spoken to you, that My joy may remain in you, and *that* your joy may be full.[133]

YHWY *Rophi* (God the Healer)

יהוה רָפָא

I have a Christian brother in Nigeria named Nedu. We have walked through fire together. He is the sort of twenty-four karat kind of person with whom you can pick up after years apart like there was no separation. Nedu has chosen to raise his family in Nigeria because he wants to serve the people there, but also sees that the spiritual atmosphere is better for his family.

In Nigeria, people come to pastors' homes starting early in the morning and keep coming late into the night. They come for help and counsel. They come for answers and assistance. One night a knock came at Nedu's door. A young mother was there with her limp son lying in her arms. She said, "My son is dying. I am a nurse and I know he is going to die tonight, but I just can't watch him die. Can I leave him with you? I just can't stand the heartbreak of losing him."

Nedu and his wife Ify took the child and the mother left. They prayed for the child through the night. Imagine the scene in the morning when the child, healed, hearty, and perfectly healthy answered the mother's knock at the door! It doesn't take any imagination to know where the child and his mother were the next

---

[133] John 15:11

171

Sunday morning. They had been evangelized by an encounter with *YHWY Rophi*, God the Healer.

The implicit question, however, is "How unusual is this kind of miracle?" For this, there is conflicting evidence. First of all, there is the experience we bring to the table. We are steeped in rational thought that says this kind of experience is a delightful fairy tale, but hardly the kind of thing that we can really expect here and now. We have the momentum of a lifetime of mediocre spiritual experience that tries to tell me things aren't going to change. The Gospels record stories of this kind of thing happening, but could it really be "normal?" Cynics say that the "stories" are the result of perhaps well-intentioned people who are trying to encourage us, but we *really know* that it is impossible.

On the other hand, we have the record of the Scriptures and the words of Jesus Himself promising that He has come "that we might have abundant life." The Isaiah passage and countless others all reinforce the same message. He is here and He is active as healer, deliverer, and King. Instead of letting my experience settle the question and leave who knows how many people bereft of grace, isn't it more reasonable to say, "God does not lie," and try to find out why my life doesn't match up with His promise?

Chapter Nine
Three Perspectives on Time
"Thy Kingdom Come, but When?"
Remember the Past
Live in the Present
Look Forward to the Future

Remembering the Past

I found myself at an evening cocktail reception at the Charleston Yacht Club. As those things develop, one can usually find conversations of some interest among the people. Some of the people's stories are fascinating. Some of the people are just plain characters. The one that sticks out in my memory was a tweed coated club member. He was wearing one of those jackets with the leather patches on the elbow. What really struck me, though, was not his dress. It was his introduction. He held out his hand and said, "My name is 'street name' 'street name.'" That was the way my wife and I had come to understand the practice of honoring prominent family connections in previous generations (who often had streets in the city named after them) by giving a newly arriving family member a blood-line family name as a first name as well as their own family moniker.

Having introduced himself, he went on, "My great, great (actually I got lost in exactly how many 'greats' he used) Uncle was so-and-so, a signer of the Declaration of Independence."

For a few moments I just stood there speechless. It was utterly amazing to me that a person would choose to share something like that as a conversation opener. As I began to recover my composure, I asked him, "What sort of contributions have you added recently to your ancestors' efforts?"

I hoped it had not sounded as insulting to him as it could have. I realized that there were lots of other things I could have asked and lots of ways I could have asked the same question with more tact.

Happily, he was not the least bit flustered. I was very taken, however, by his reply. With a deep "Southun" drawl he swirled a glass of whiskey and ice and replied, "Ah have fulfilled mah responsibility to the blood line…Ah have produced a male heir."

His voice indicated a deep seriousness with almost a religious tone. He defined his existence from what had been done in the past. His contribution was to provide a male heir that could carry on the family. As much of the world outside Charleston (and some other deep south cities) has pretty much moved on from this kind of purely historical perspective, his focus may seem strange, but it actually reflects the reverence with which we look back on the work of Jesus in our lives. In the same way, our challenge is to live effectively to pass on that life to the next generation.

We need to know not only what Jesus has done, but also how those who have been committed to Him have lived as well. There is a great deal to learn from them.

Living in the Present

The heart of what it means to "live in the present" is having Christ-centered and spiritually ordered relationships. We get a clue as to the standard of relationships when we read the High Priestly Prayer of Jesus.

> "I do not pray for these alone, but also for those who will believe in Me through their word; 21 that they all may be one, as You,

Father, *are* in Me, and I in You; that they also may be one in Us, that the world may believe that You sent Me.[134]

Notice that we are called to mirror the unity that is found in the Trinity. The foundation of this is clearly that we are in Christ and in belief. Relationships are then built through serving and treating each other with honor.

> *Let* love *be* without hypocrisy. Abhor what is evil. Cling to what is good. 10 *Be* kindly affectionate to one another with brotherly love, in honor giving preference to one another; 11 not lagging in diligence, fervent in spirit, serving the Lord; 12 rejoicing in hope, patient in tribulation, continuing steadfastly in prayer; 13 distributing to the needs of the saints, given to hospitality. 14 Bless those who persecute you; bless and do not curse. 15 Rejoice with those who rejoice, and weep with those who weep. 16 Be of the same mind toward one another.[135]

To make how we relate to each other clear, the New Testament has more than five hundred verses about "one another."

Looking Forward to the Future
While we may not know every detail of how things will play out in our lives, we live with a great advantage. God has revealed His grand scheme: He wins and He shares His victory with us! Even if we have struggles, *ultimately* we will have victory.

---

[134] John 17:20-21
[135] Romans 12:1-16

175

But in all *things* we commend ourselves as ministers of God: in much patience, in tribulations, in needs, in distresses, 5 in stripes, in imprisonments, in tumults, in labors, in sleeplessness, in fastings; 6 by purity, by knowledge, by longsuffering, by kindness, by the Holy Spirit, by sincere love, 7 by the word of truth, by the power of God, by the armor of righteousness on the right hand and on the left, 8 by honor and dishonor, by evil report and good report; as deceivers, and *yet* true; 9 as unknown, and *yet* well known; as dying, and behold we live; as chastened, and *yet* not killed; 10 as sorrowful, yet always rejoicing; as poor, yet making many rich; as having nothing, and *yet* possessing all things.[136]

Temporal and material things can be taken away. We can suffer and may even be martyred, but our victory in Christ cannot be taken away. St. Augustine wrote about it in the fifth century when people began to ask questions about those who had earthly belongings taken by force. He makes it clear that our eternal inheritance is of much greater value.

For nothing could perish on earth save what they would be ashamed to carry away from earth.[137]

In Kingdom terms, we can run full out without a net. Well, actually without any other net than Jesus Himself. It gives us a whole new

---

[136] 2 Corinthians 6:4-10

[137] Philip Schaff, ed. *A Select Library of the Nicene and Post-Nicene Fathers of the Christian Church, ed Volume II: St. Augustine's City of God* (Eerdmans, Chicago, 1957), page 8.

perspective on the present when we know our future so clearly. Again, thinking of the Möbius Strip, we live today *and* we live in and for tomorrow. Both are true.

Chapter Ten
Three Ways of Kingdom Economics
Kingdom Economics–Faith and Provision

Give us This Day our Daily Bread...
Kingdom View
Widows Mite
5 Loaves / 2 Fish

Dealing with Money and Things.

There is a great reminder that we have fallen short of the eternal existence that the Creator originally sang into us before The Fall. Every day we need bread. Every day we have a reminder that we are frail and mortal. Every day there is a demanding call from inside us that craves attention. At some level, we know that if we fail to address it, we will soon grow too weak. Eventually we will die for lack.

When Jesus taught "His" prayer to the disciples (and consequently every succeeding generation) He was teaching us to commend our frail existence into the Father's care. For those (like in the Western industrial nations) who live with abundance, our reliance on His provision is not as obvious. Some who labor close to the land know how fragile provision can be. Many gloss over our dependence on the goodness of God and amass what for most of the world looks to be a huge stockpile of resources, but the fact is, there are ways in which we are really frail. Withhold food for too many weeks and the body faints and eventually dies. A week without water and even the strongest will be at the brink of death. A few minutes without oxygen and life is ended.

It's not that God wants to end our lives. On the contrary, He wants us to come to Him and live forever. He does, however, want us to recognize our dependence on Him. People of the Kingdom live in a rhythm of dependence and provision that is repeated day after day.

For some, the thread is barely visible. If circumstances are generous, then bountiful resources surround us. For much of the world, however, it is a struggle to survive. Finding food every single day can be challenging, burdensome, or even depressing.

So, Jesus asks us to pray. He wants us to ask the Father to provide. That is not because we have to convince Him to give us what we need. It is to help us realize who we are and Who He is. It is easy to forget.

There is a wonderful window into the Kingdom. It is in Romans, where Paul is writing intensely about faith, but it goes far beyond that. It is a place where God reveals more about our destiny than perhaps in any other passage.

> Therefore *it is* of faith that *it might be* according to grace, so that the promise might be sure to all the seed, not only to those who are of the law, but also to those who are of the faith of Abraham, who is the father of us all 17 (as it is written, *"I have made you a father of many nations"*) in the presence of Him whom he believed—God, who gives life to the dead and calls those things which do not exist as though they did; 18 who, contrary to hope, in hope believed, so that he became the father of many nations, according to what was spoken, *"So shall your descendants be."* 19 And not being weak in faith, he did not consider his own body, already dead (since he was about a hundred years old), and the deadness of Sarah's womb. 20 He did not waver at the promise of God through

unbelief, but was strengthened in faith, giving glory to God, 21 and being fully convinced that what He had promised He was also able to perform. 22 And therefore *"it was accounted to him for righteousness."[138]*

For God to see things that are not yet as though they are, means that He sees things that *are* before we do—long before they *are* for us. He prepares them for us, longing for us to pluck them out of heaven's storehouse where they have been destined and wait for us. This is part of what it means to be "predestined." The provision has been provided before we knew the need for it. It is earmarked and prepared for us. It is ready and in a sense, waiting for us.

Many people falter when they pray, falsely thinking that they must pray something into being "from scratch." It seems to be too hard to pray for a resource to be created. In fact it is easy to stall when we don't know the answers, but God does not demand that we know everything. He is looking for something else. That something else is strangled by arrogance. So the Lord speaks to us (as He did to Job):

> Then the LORD answered Job out of the whirlwind, and said:
> "Who *is* this who darkens counsel
> By words without knowledge?
> Now prepare yourself like a man;
> I will question you, and you shall answer Me.
> "Where were you when I laid the foundations of the earth?
> Tell *Me,* if you have understanding.
> Who determined its measurements?
> Surely you know!
> Or who stretched the line upon it?

---

[138] Romans 4:16-22

To what were its foundations fastened?
Or who laid its cornerstone,
When the morning stars sang together,
And all the sons of God shouted for joy?[139]

Get the picture? We are **not** in charge. We spend a lot of time and energy *trying* to be, but we're not.

God thunders marvelously with His voice;
He does great things which we cannot comprehend.
For He says to the snow, "Fall *on* the earth';
Likewise to the gentle rain and the heavy rain of His strength. He seals the hand of every man,
That all men may know His work.[140]

Welcome to God's reality. Every snowflake that will ever fall exists in God's presence. Every raindrop and every hailstone. That is an amazing revelation, but that is only the start. In fact, *everything* we will ever need already exists in His heavenly storehouse. Everything.

Imagine if "daily bread" actually extends to all that we need; every provision, every meal, and every resource. Imagine if this actually extends to wisdom, courage, guidance, and even healing. All those needs are not surprises to which God wakes when our prayers invade His celestial slumbers. Needs are anticipated—every one of them. The resources to meet the needs do not have to be created in some sort of emergency provision factory that is fueled by fervent intercession. Our prayers can simply be a way for the circumstances of our lives to line up with the vision God has for what can be. Provision, rather than being the eventual fruit of

---

[139] Job 38:2-7
[140] Job 37:5-7

exhausting birth-pang prayer, can be instead God's children doing things God's way.

To get a grip on understanding intercessory prayer, one of the best resources available is Dutch Sheets book, *Intercessory Prayer*. I highly recommend making it part of your personal library. It is simply filled with insights and illumination of what is possible in Christ. He writes:

> When we intercede, cooperating with the Spirit of God, it releases Him to go out from us and hover over a situation, releasing His life-birthing energies until that which we are asking for comes forth.[141]

Jesus does this all the time. When He says, "You are the salt of the earth," or "You are the light of the world," He is not so foolish as to think that all the circumstances of our lives here already line up with saltiness. He is saying that He sees us as we "more truly" are. He sees us, not bound in time and weighed down by sin's shortcomings. He sees us as we will be when we are with Him. That reality is as real to Him today as it will be when we are birthed into eternity. Creation waits, longs, and groans in birth pangs for what will be. He sees tomorrow as we see today. We live burdened down with the weight of limited vision of only being able to see the present and trying to remember the past. In the heavenly storehouse the future already *is*. He sees us in the storehouse, salty, and luminous. When God looks at us here, it is with the confidence that comes from knowing how things will turn out. With lavish generosity, He prays provision down on us so our circumstances begin to line up with heaven's reality. It was

---

[141] Dutch Sheets, *Intercessory Prayer*, (Ventura, CA: Regal, 1996), page 206.

predestined. It was designed. It was prepared for us, and it is raining down for "whosoever will."

Intercession is one of the great currencies of the Kingdom. It's not that there is some sort of heavenly inertia that has to be overcome in order to convince a grumpy and stodgy God to act. He is, in fact, more willing to answer than we are to pray.

I love the imagery that there are bowls in heaven that are filled with the prayers of the saints (that's *us* of course).[142] Every time we pray, every intercession, every act of praise, every prayer of worship—imagine these bowls being filled. Surely, if there are bowls that can pour out wrath and suffering, angels are there who can stir up the contents of the bowls so healing and grace flows just as it did from the pool of Bethesda.[143] [144] I remember Dutch Sheets saying, "Suppose God moves to tip the bowl, and there is too little in it." What a motivation to pray!

I'm not thrilled to say how many times I've either failed to pray at all, or have pretty much just gone through the motions. There is another kind of prayer. It is a "birthing" prayer; one of such intensity that it yearns, calls, and longs for something to happen. Although I'd be quick to admit that my wife's part was significantly more difficult than mine, I was there when both our daughters were born. It was a monumental, even Herculean effort on her part. For our first born, labor was intense and long…thirty-one hours to be exact. The fruit of the labor, however, was magnificent: our daughter. Surely we would see more fruit if we prayed like that, with deep groaning and straining.

---

[142] Revelation 5:8
[143] Revelation 16:2
[144] John 5:1

> And Elijah went up to the top of Carmel; then he
> bowed down on the ground, and put his face between
> his knees, <u>43</u> and said to his servant, "Go up now,
> look toward the sea." So he went up and looked, and
> said, "*There is* nothing." And seven times he said, "Go
> again."
> Then it came to pass the seventh *time,* that he said,
> "There is a cloud, as small as a man's hand, rising out
> of the sea!" So he said, "Go up, say to Ahab, 'Prepare
> *your chariot,* and go down before the rain stops
> you.' "[145]

Elijah's prayer was a birthing prayer. Look at the way he bent over, put his face between his knees and *worked* at prayer.

Notice three things about that prayer. First, he prayed with great intensity. Second, he didn't stop until he saw something happen. Third, when he saw the tiniest change, he knew that God was answering. Even though there was only a cloud the size of a man's hand, Elijah saw a cloudburst in the making. He told King Ahab to get moving before the rain overwhelmed him. That's confidence.

Giving with a Glad Heart

Money in the Kingdom doesn't work like money in the world. Gold and silver have intrinsic value. Paper money stands for something. In the United States, it used to stand for silver, now it stands for a promise from the government. In worldly terms, the "glory" of money expresses the value attached to other things, be they time, services, or material goods.

In the Kingdom, however, it works differently. In Ghana, they speak of "sweet money" and "bitter money." It has to do with the

---

[145] 1 Kings 18:42bf

heart attitude of how the money is acquired and how it is used. Unrighteous "bitter money" will not bring positive fruit. Dishonest activities may generate large sums of money, but it will come with a hole in the purse. Oh, there may be temporal success—even abundance—but it cannot last. For a time, evil can prosper and it seems that the Kingdom is not robust enough to enforce its rules. Josh McDowell teaches that negative moral choices have a temporary positive result but a long term negative result. In contrast, positive moral choices have a preliminary negative consequence but a positive one in the long run.[146]

For example, if I choose an extra piece of chocolate cake, there is an immediate reward: the cake. The negative long-term impact is the toll that it takes on my waistline. Conversely, forgoing the cake has a negative immediate consequence: No cake! But a long term positive. Choose any arena and the principle is the same: sexuality, integrity, courage, honesty, or self-sacrifice. It all works the same. The framework of the Kingdom of God cannot be thwarted. Money that is given with bad motives has the same problem. It will not buy the fruit of the Spirit. Gifts given to God grudgingly or for show will not advance the Kingdom, either.

Nigerian Christians (especially the Igbo tribe) have the practice of dancing to expressive choruses during the offering. They line up and dance their way to an offering basket at the front of the church. The cathedral in Onitsha is one of the largest church buildings in Africa. It is so huge it seems to have its own weather system inside. Imagine thousands of people moving rhythmically, coming with joy to return to God some of His provision to them. Often dressed in their "Sunday best," dancing at the offering can be expressive—even extravagant. I recall the pastor of the cathedral enjoining the people, "Let your offering reflect your dance and your dance reflect your offering."

---

[146] Josh McDowell, *Right from Wrong* (Word Waco 1994) page 171.

In other words, a generous or sacrificial gift deserves a generous dance. An elaborate dance deserves a commensurate offering!

If you imagine that offering dances are an outward portrayal of the interior condition of the heart, there is a great deal of truth in what he said. Paul wrote, "*So let* each one *give* as he purposes in his heart, not grudgingly or of necessity; for God loves a cheerful giver."[147]

The Greek word for cheerful is actually ʹιλαρον *hilaron* (same root as *hilarious*) giver. What makes a gift hilarious? A glad heart. A celebrative spirit. Expectancy, thankfulness, abandon, and a life filled with trust and thanksgiving toward God.

To bear fruit for the Kingdom and in our lives, our tithes and offerings rise out of our relationship with God as provider, redeemer, and friend. Rather than trying to pare down our giving to the minimum level possible, the *hilarious* heart will ask, "How much *can* I give?"

How the world views money vs the Kingdom view

If you stay up late at night and turn on the TV one of the things you see besides trashy (yet strangely still very expensive!) exercise equipment are infomercials touting books, CD's, seminars, and DVD's that show the "secrets" of acquiring wealth. Besides the unbelievable, there are some legitimate principles that emerge. Interestingly, the ones that work are the same ones that are taught in business schools. The New Testament, however, teaches different principles. The Bible teaches us how to build things that will have lasting value.

---

[147] 2 Corinthians 9:7

Many of the principles of Kingdom economics are directly at odds with the way we have experienced business in the world.

Business Man's Way	Business God's Way
Use Other Peoples Money	Five loaves and two fish
Maximize Profits	What does it profit?
Me first	The greatest serve
Compounding	Multiplied Harvest
Pay yourself first	Pay (return to) God first
Trust the tangible	Trust what can't be seen
Deal increasingly sharply	Better and better wine
Maintain control	Surrender to God
Use debt	Avoid debt
Use things intensely	Time to lie fallow
Perception is reality	Reality is reality
Consume and acquire	Give (hilariously)
Instant gratification	Deferred gratification

In each case, the Kingdom way is either a direct reversal of the "secular" presumptions people bring to business, or they are a magnificent extrapolation of temporal concepts.

The Widow's Mite

I was speaking at St. James Cathedral in Kasase, Uganda. Most of the people didn't speak any English, so I was preaching with an interpreter. Uganda is a beautiful country, but poverty is rampant. The per capita income is only about $300 per year. That is quite unfathomable to westerners. On this occasion, however, I wasn't there as a rich American. I came needy. The church was packed with people who had very little money, but they were rich in everything eternal. They knew the joy of the Lord's salvation. They were convinced Christians, filled with power, prayer, and evangelistic zeal. I told them that the church in the US had a lot of money, but it is poor in the currency of the Kingdom. I preached on

188

the Macedonian call and said that we needed their help. We needed to learn from them.

At the close of the sermon, the pastor of the church got up and spoke in the local language. My interpreter leaned over to me and whispered what was being said. The pastor said, "Our brothers and sisters in America are asking for our help." With amazing generosity of spirit he continued, "When brothers in Christ ask for help, we have a responsibility to help. Raise your hand if you are willing to help."

He went on, "I want you to understand. When your brothers and sisters in Christ ask for your help, you don't say, 'Send me a ticket and I will help you.' We have a responsibility. I am challenging this congregation to equip at least one evangelist to go from our congregation to America, and I'm challenging the people of this church to pay for it. Now…who is willing to help? Who is willing to give? We're going to have an extra offering right now to start raising money."

The ushers responded right away, moving through the congregation. It was obvious that "extra" offerings were not unusual to these people, but it was an unusual offering. In addition to money being dropped into the offering bags there was a shirt and two wooden spoons. There was also a small bowl of peanuts. My interpreter said, "Some people are giving things because they want to participate, but they don't have *any* money."

What happened next was even more amazing. When the service concluded, a table was brought out to the center aisle. The lay leader of the congregation (called the *warden*) took a seat behind it. He proceeded to hold an auction for the gifts that were not money. He sold the shirt and the spoons to the highest bidder and then held up the bowl of peanuts (they call them "ground nuts" in Africa). They may have been worth ten or twenty cents, but a

189

businessman was willing to pay 1000 shillings for them. At the time, that was almost a dollar. But the really interesting thing came next. An acolyte took the bowl of peanuts over to the businessman. He opened his handkerchief and poured the peanuts into it. Then, without even looking back, he passed the bowl over his shoulder. In each row, the person who received the bowl did the same as it got passed farther and farther back.

My interpreter said, "Watch this," as it continued to be passed back all the way to a widow sitting on the last row.

"What is going on?" I asked. "What are they doing with the bowl?"

Somberly, he replied, "She wanted to give something so she gave the ground nuts, but that is her only bowl."

I had surely seen the widow's mite. And what extravagant fruit it is bearing.

"Five Loaves and Two Fish"

> 12 When the day began to wear away, the twelve came and said to Him, "Send the multitude away, that they may go into the surrounding towns and country, and lodge and get provisions; for we are in a deserted place here."
> Luke 9:13 But He said to them, "You give them something to eat."
> And they said, "We have no more than five loaves and two fish, unless we go and buy food for all these people."
> 14 For there were about five thousand men.
> Then He said to His disciples, "Make them sit down in groups of fifty." 15 And they did so, and made them all sit down.

Luke 9:16 Then He took the five loaves and the two fish, and looking up to heaven, He blessed and broke *them*, and gave *them* to the disciples to set before the multitude. 17 So they all ate and were filled, and twelve baskets of the leftover fragments were taken up by them.[148]

1 "Ho! Everyone who thirsts,
Come to the waters;
And you who have no money,
Come, buy and eat.
Yes, come, buy wine and milk
Without money and without price.[149]

---

[148] Luke 9:12-17
[149] Isaiah 55:1

Chapter Eleven
Three Freedoms of the Kingdom
Forgiveness
Freedom
Transformation

Forgive us our trespasses as we forgive those who trespass against us...
Forgiveness: A two-way street

The day before I was going to be ordained I went to see a priest named Jim Radebaugh. He has long since gone on to be with the Lord, but at the time he was well known for his wisdom in giving spiritual direction. He had a knack for asking a question or making a surgical statement that would penetrate right into the heart of a thorny problem. I went to see him because I was mad. I was bitter-angry at someone who had unjustly hurt me and I wanted to ask Jim about it. Worse than that, I knew I couldn't be ordained with the level of bitterness I had in my heart. Even though I had been innocent in the events surrounding a series of attacks on my ministry, I was on the verge of being obsessed with anger toward the man who was the principle one who had hurt me. It was so out of order I remember thinking, "If I present myself for ordination without dealing with this, the Lord would be justified in just striking me dead."

I poured out my heart to Jim and told him how hurt, angry, and disappointed I was at the adverse circumstances and the injustice that had been done to me. Jim was an unusual priest. He had been brought up on a ranch and had been a rodeo cowboy, excelling in bull riding. Bull riding is in my view not even borderline insanity, but without a doubt such *totally* manly stuff that is intimidating to mere mortals. I opened up the conversation over coffee at the town square café in the little place he lived by asking about his time in the rodeo.

"Is it true you used to ride bulls?"

"I don't do that no more," he said dismissively in a totally cowboy (but absolutely authentic) accent. "Some folks think it's 'cuz I got tired of falling off. Ain't so. I quit 'cuz I got tired o' hittin' the ground. But ridin' bulls ain't why you came to see me."

"No," I admitted. "I came because I know I can't get ordained with the anger I have in my heart toward a guy who tried to destroy my ministry. And he darn near succeeded." As we drank coffee, I poured out my heart and a river of hurt, anger, and pain.

When I finished describing what had happened, how I had been wronged, and how I wanted to end the bitterness, Jim drawled, "The problem with unforgiveness is that it messes you up. You're walking around stewin' all the time about this guy and he don't ever even think of you. You're the prisoner and he don't even care about you. Forgiveness means lettin' him off scott-free fer what he did…releasing him from havin' to pay for it. The funny thing is, though, that it's you that gets free."

As he spoke I knew it was the truth. I needed to loose and forgive the man who had hurt me so deeply, but I was the one that had been in bondage. As I said that I would release him, something dramatic shifted inside me. I was actually the one who was set free.

Release the offender, so you can be released

In the Lord 's Prayer, Jesus taught, "Forgive us our trespasses as we forgive those who trespass against us." Forgiving and being forgiven are inexorably tied together. That's not just a technicality that God set up to make life more challenging for us. The reason is that there is a single "forgiveness door" in our hearts. Giving forgiveness and receiving forgiveness both have to flow through the same door. If I refuse to forgive, there is no portal for forgiveness to enter my life. My repentance is a central part of my forgiveness. In Kingdom terms, the restoration of one who has offended me is not just a nice thing to do. It is absolutely key to the Abundant Life that Jesus speaks about for both of us.

In 2005, I was invited to speak at the 70th Anniversary Celebration of the East African revival. The revival began when a group of indigenous missionaries from Rwanda came across the border to Kabale, Uganda to teach at the Bishop Barham College. As they shared the Gospel and taught about the power of God, the Holy Spirit fell powerfully on the group. They were so dramatically impacted that everyone there went out preaching and calling people to repentance. Now, every ten years, more than ten thousand people come to an open-air gathering to remember and carry on the preaching tradition. Though they are now very old, a few of the original people who were there "when the fire fell" are still alive and still bear powerful testimony to the Gospel. One old man looked frail and bent over his cane until joyful worship and praise choruses broke out. With a magnificent grin on his face he lifted his cane over his head and danced to the rhythmic singing.

Recently, I saw the power of repentance, forgiveness, and release manifest when I received a call from a man who had been extremely angry with me for years. He had said I had wronged him and refused to have any conversation about it. It is practically impossible to be reconciled when there is no contact.

As he battled with a series of surgeries, something moved in him. Perhaps it was the impending sense of his mortality. After not hearing anything from him for years I received a call asking me to visit him in the hospital not really knowing what to expect. When I walked into the room, his eyes immediately filled with tears and he began to sob. He cried out, "I have wronged you. I have harbored ill will against you. I have been arrogant and bitter and I have been wrong. Will you forgive me? Will you pray with me for God to forgive me? I don't want to live like this any more. I want a new life!"

We cried together as I held him and I watched God's power to redeem and transform.

Rarely have I ever witnessed such deep repentance. When it happens, it is a profound and a holy thing. One of the great, historic priestly ministries in The Church is the declaration of the forgiveness of sins. It is widely misunderstood. It's not that the priest forgives the sin. The priest's job is to give assurance to those who have confessed sin to God that He forgives repentant sinners declaring,

"God desires not the death of a sinner, but that the sinner turn from his evil ways and live."[150]

Of course we can confess things to God and be forgiven without anyone else around, but sometimes it is extremely helpful to have another person who can say, "Yes. You did what Jesus asks and have confessed your sin and repented. The Bible says that you are forgiven." That's what "absolution" is all about.

It was remarkable to watch someone be transformed in a hospital bed. As he was releasing me, he experienced a freedom he had never known before. By the time I left the room, he had the fresh life of a newborn baby. I had watched God do His most magnificent miracle. When we are privileged to see something like that, we should take stock of our own lives to see where we have the same bondage.

---

[150] The Prayer of Absolution, *The Book of Common Prayer*.

The Five Part Forgiveness Prayer

Working through forgiveness when you have been wounded can be more difficult than it sounds. The biggest reason is that when we have been wronged it can be very painful. Even if I want to release the other person, I may still be in pain from the wound that was inflicted. My wife shared this five-step "Forgiveness Prayer" with me that she had put together. In my completely objective opinion, it is the best model I have ever seen to work through the issues of forgiveness.

The Five Part Forgiveness Prayer

1. Pray to declare forgiveness for the person and ask God to change your heart towards them.

2. Pray to be healed of the wound their sin caused you.

3. Pray for double honor for the shame they caused you (Isaiah 61:7).

4. Pray to be forgiven of judgments you made about/against them as a result of their actions against you and extend mercy.

5. Pray for God to Bless them.[151]

Notice, that like the Möbius Strip, God is addressing things both in us and others. He is efficient that way.

Sadly, unforgiveness is not the only way that we bind people. We often do it with expectations or with pronouncements we make

---

[151] Susan Atwood, "The Five Part Forgiveness Prayer." © 2006

over other people's lives. One of the most common places this happens is with parents and children. While affirmations can be encouraging, many parents make the terrible mistake of labeling their children in negative ways that bind them.

Transfiguration

When we say that something is transformed we mean that it is experiencing change for good. Transformation is about things becoming better, but there is a greater glory. It is called Transfiguration. Transfiguration is the miraculous process in which wounds actually become beautiful. To those who don't know the outcome, the Cross is a terrible and terrifying instrument of torture. Of course it is that, but it is so much more. The wounds on the body of Jesus are terrible, too, but now that we know "the rest of the story," we see His victory over all the suffering. Now, we see the love that motivated Him and the power that is manifest in his rising. Wounds that were sources of sadness before, now become trophies of love and His victory. Those wounds no longer cause Him pain. Instead they are evidence of His love for us. The nail prints and spear wound now no longer bleed, but they cry out that we are loved and He is victorious.

Perhaps the key in transfiguration is that the wound is *offered*. Jesus was willing to lay down everything on our behalf. While we cannot effect the redemption of others, we can *affect* it! We can offer our wounds to Him for His use. When we do so out of love for Him and for others, something happens to the wounds and scars. Not only does the hurt ebb, a great impact for good can rise. When we offer our wounds and scars to Jesus and then to others, He bears fruit. Of course, it is only Jesus who redeems, but honest sharing about what we have been through and have done, and how He has forgiven and healed us, expands his glory.

This is not to say that God sends us suffering. Everything that comes from God is good, because He is good.[152] Always remember it is the devil who seeks to steal, kill, and destroy. Without question, however, God can use things that have brought us anguish and transfigure them so that they bring joy.

---

[152] James 1:17

Chapter Twelve

Three Struggles

War in Heaven
Warriors in Heaven
Strategies for Warfare

Lead us not into temptation, but deliver us from evil...
War in Heaven!

> "How you are fallen from heaven,
> O Lucifer, son of the morning!
> How you are cut down to the ground,
> You who weakened the nations!
> For you have said in your heart:
> "I will ascend into heaven,
> I will exalt my throne above the stars of God;
> I will also sit on the mount of the congregation
> On the farthest sides of the north;
> I will ascend above the heights of the clouds,
> I will be like the Most High.'
> Yet you shall be brought down to Sheol,
> To the lowest depths of the Pit.
> "Those who see you will gaze at you,
> And consider you, saying:
> 'Is this the man who made the earth tremble, who shook
> kingdoms,[153]

Even before the terrible day in the garden when the serpent deceived Eve, there was a war in heaven. It was short-lived and *very* one-sided, but it was a war nevertheless. Lucifer (*The Light-bearer*) was the most beautiful of all the angels. On the surface, the

---

[153] Isaiah 14:12-16

narrative in Isaiah speaks of the ruin of the King of Babylon; however, it is not difficult to see it as being even more applicable to Satan himself, the Fallen Angel, and all the spiritual beings that revolted with him.

At the very instant he purposed rebellion in his heart, judgment came like a thunderclap. Lucifer fell from his exalted position as the administrator of Heaven into a far less beautiful and not so glamorous state. Now as a fallen spirit-being, he is bent on destruction and acts as the tormentor committed to destroying our lives.

Tradition suggests that one third of the angels fell with him, but the exact number is not particularly important. In any case, he and his minions struck a great blow in the Garden. It was all-out war on his part in an attempt to subvert creation and drag us away from God into perdition. That plan, conceived in the Garden, continues to this day.

From what was created by God to reflect and share His glory, the fallen kingdom looks very much like it, but is the awful, mirror image. It is the functional opposite of what God has created. Though the Scriptures are not explicit, it appears that some of each type of spiritual being fell. The result is a devilish, perverse, fallen government that stands at odds with God and the purpose for whichever Christian has been created and redeemed.

In generation after generation, the forces of Hell are marshaled by their evil general to assault the people God has created for fellowship and purpose. Those who come to Scripture's promises know that the devil's end is sure and the victory of Jesus is absolute. We do, however, have to walk through many battles. It does help, though, to know Who wins.

For this purpose the Son of God was manifested, that He might *destroy* the works of the devil.[154] [155]

That destruction is coming and his end is guaranteed. For now, though,

> Be sober; be vigilant; because your adversary the devil walks about like a roaring lion, seeking whom he may devour.[156]

We have no need to fear the devil if we are in Christ, *and* we remain steadfastly committed to do God's will. But he can inflict great damage if we refuse to recognize the sphere of influence where he still operates. A priest's wife called me recently to ask me if she was being unreasonable to be upset with her husband. Several times a week, he was spending time alone with women in the parish. In the same week he had gone to lunch with one (just the two of them) and gone for martinis with another. When she asked him about it he dismissed it as "purely professional," and of "no concern." Speaking of the area of fidelity and sexuality, he told her, "In that area, I am bullet proof. You have nothing to worry about." One of the most tragic choices that a Christian can make is looking to see how close to the edge they can walk, rather than fleeing from evil (or what can quickly turn into evil). The underlying assumption is that *"fun"* and satisfaction are found in the world, rather than in the Lord. While the Scriptures are clear that there may be pleasure in sin *for a season*, the eventual fruit will be bitter indeed.

Those captivated by the heart and Kingdom of God will seek to conform their lives to His word. Of course there is a cost to do that,

---

[154] 1 John 3:8b
[155] Strong's Concordance 1847 . ἐξουδενεω exoudeneo; from 1537 and 3762; *to despise, set at nought:* —treated with contempt(1).
[156] 1 Peter 5:8

but the fruit is sweeter than can be described. When we live by God's ordinances, there isn't any concern with being caught, either.

I could tell that she was a rather frightened clergy spouse. She asked me what she could say to her husband, particularly since she had already tried and failed to influence him.

When I prayed over the phone with the upset wife, I had the strong sense that the image he needed to understand was that his actions were aggravating the wound in an already painful part of her life. What he was doing might not have pierced the spirit of someone else in other circumstances, but for those with abandonment issues, it was very painful and very difficult to deal with. He wasn't aware that he was being used by dark spiritual forces. Equally, he was not aware that much damage had been done.

It is quite remarkable that the fallen dark kingdom parallels the Kingdom of God so closely. Fallen angels are on assignments. They are spirits that seek to subvert and corrupt the opposite of the way that God's holy angels call us to holiness.

The Kingdom of Heaven	**The Dark Kingdom**
Archangels	Lucifer and Fallen Archangels
Angels (Messengers of Truth)	Deceiving Messenger angels
Cherubim (Guard the Holy)	Promote unholy behavior
Seraphim (Declare "Holy!")	Declare blasphemies
Thrones (Seat of Holiness)	Seats of Demonic activity
Powers (How God works)	Dark Powers of Evil
Principalities (How God Rules)	Dark Princes
Dominions (Order)	Dark Places of Rebellion
Virtues (Promote virtue)	Vices (Seduce people into vices)

While the evil one seeks only to steal, kill, and destroy, the Father invites us into lives of Abundance, Conquering, and Creativity. Notice that Satan attacks the very things God has put in order. Though He didn't have to, God has chosen to "administrate" His

Kingdom through the workings of angelic beings. While the Scriptures are not absolutely explicit about all the roles of all the angels, we can get a good idea of who they are and something of how they work.

Though in contrast to the God of order, Satan is a promoter of chaos. That does not mean that it is impossible to determine any patterns in the way the devil operates. Remember that he is committed *only* to steal, kill, and destroy. If those things are present, look around for the Evil One. Any time there is *torment* there is a good chance evil forces are about. There are also discernable patterns of the sorts of attacks he will wage. Since he is not creative, he will very often resort to attacks in similar patterns. When you encounter a pattern of similar attacks, it is likely that dark forces are at the heart of it. When we see the dark prince working, we should resist him. Not only is he no match for God's power, he is actually defeated. Jesus Christ's victory on the Cross is complete. It may take some time for the victory to be fully manifest, but it will come; that is sure.

Angels and Archangels
Angels, of course, are heavenly messengers. Archangels rule over them and oversee major areas of their ministries. As awesome as their power is, even they will defer to a Greater Power when necessary.

> Yet Michael the archangel, in contending with the devil, when he disputed about the body of Moses, dared not bring against him a reviling accusation, but said, "The Lord rebuke you!"[157]

---

[157] Jude 9

God's Order	Satan's Attacks
Providing Abundance	Stealing
Dominion for Life	Killing
Creativity	Destroying

God, in His mercy, provides us not only an escape from the eternal fate that Satan will have, He invites us into a life that mirrors His own. Jesus describes it as "abundant life."[158] Whatever that means to Him, it is a sure thing that it is good. It is rich, rewarding, and (no surprise) *abundant*. Tragically, relatively few people are actually living an abundant life.

Though redemption will rescue many people from the devil, he is very effective in his evil work. What started in the garden continues to soil our innocence, rob us of intimacy with the Father, and pollute our purpose.

The Fall was a ghastly event, but its impact is actually even worse than it looks at first. The very people who had been created to have intimate fellowship with God were set in a rebellion that we could not repair. Not only that, but each generation's rebellion inflicts new wounds as the sins of the fathers are visited on the next generation.

No matter how finely dressed, richly adorned, or fervently ignored, the stench of sin wrecked our experience of *everything*. This is not to say that the Father ever ceased loving us, but we were in such a bad place we couldn't experience it.

Seraphim, Cherubim, and Thrones

Surrounding the throne of God are Cherubim, Seraphim, and Thrones. Cherubim serve as the guards of the Kingdom, guarding the garden, the Throne of God, and whatever else God dispatches

---

[158] John 10:10

them to guard.[159] The principal role of the Seraphim is to surround the Throne of God with praise.[160]

Thrones are not only seats, but they are also "seats of power;" places from which leadership in the Kingdom is exercised. The ancient church picked up on this by naming the chair where the local bishop sits as the *"cathedra"*, which is Latin for the bishop's chair from which he leads. It draws from the victory of Jesus where:

> ...the God of our Lord Jesus Christ, the Father of glory, may give to you the spirit of wisdom and revelation in the knowledge of Him, 18 the eyes of your understanding being enlightened; that you may know what is the hope of His calling, what are the riches of the glory of His inheritance in the saints, 19 and what *is* the exceeding greatness of His power toward us who believe, according to the working of His mighty power 20 which He worked in Christ when He raised Him from the dead and seated *Him* at His right hand in the heavenly *places*, 21 far above all principality and power and might and dominion, and every name that is named, not only in this age but also in that which is to come.[161]

Powers
"Powers" exist, not surprisingly, to manifest the Power of God.

> ...now the manifold wisdom of God might be made known by the church to the principalities and powers in the heavenly *places*, 11 according to the eternal purpose which He accomplished in Christ Jesus our Lord, 12 in

---

[159] Genesis 3:22
[160] Isaiah 6:1-3
[161] Ephesians 1:17-21

whom we have boldness and access with confidence through faith in Him.[162]

Notice how the manifestation of the Power of God works to our benefit. When His power works in us, on us, or through us, it serves the "eternal purpose" accomplished in Christ Jesus. Best of all, when its strength is focused on principalities unseen (but still very *real*) it confirms not only Who He is, but Whose we are. Fallen powers seek to manifest evil power to distort and disrupt. They are the mirror image of the Power of good angelic beings—exactly, totally, completely evilly backward. This would include things like destructive miracles but could also be seen in the wizardry of Jannes and Jambrese contending with Moses before Pharoah.[163]

Principalities

Principalities (like Princes) rule over things. They may do so by decree or by force, but their strength comes from God and serving His purpose. The dark principalities that have rebelled against God and assault our lives are no match for the power of Jesus. When He challenges them, they crumble and their power over us is humiliated.

> In Him you were also circumcised with the circumcision made without hands, by putting off the body of the sins of the flesh, by the circumcision of Christ, 12 buried with Him in baptism, in which you also were raised with *Him* through faith in the working of God, who raised Him from the dead. 13 And you, being dead in your trespasses and the uncircumcision of your flesh, He has made alive together with Him, having forgiven you all trespasses, 14 having wiped out the handwriting of requirements that was against us, which was contrary to

---

[162] Ephesians 3:10-12
[163] Exodus 7, 2 Timothy 3:8

us. And He has taken it out of the way, having nailed it to the cross. <u>15</u> Having disarmed principalities and powers, He made a public spectacle of them, triumphing over them in it.[164]

Dark principalities are like evil princes who subvert justice and flout the law. It is not hard to envision them in the heart of lawless neighborhoods or in communities that are rife with crime. In fact, one of the fruits of dark principalities operating is chaos. Hebrew is a wonderful language to describe chaos. The Hebrew term is תֹהוּ *tohu*. It can mean a whole range of awful things: chaos, confusion, desolation, emptiness, empty space, formless, futile, futile things, meaningless, meaningless arguments, nothing, waste, or waste place. Basically, none of those things have anything to do with God's Kingdom and the fruit it produces.

It should be clear, however, that things like confusion and meaningless arguments will have to be ejected if we are to come into the peace of the Kingdom. The experience and reports of many intercessors is that principalities are more like personalities than vague, generic forces like the tide.

Dominions
The word "dominion" comes from the Latin for *Lord- **Dominus***. The Greek term for dominion, **κυριότης** *kuriotes*; is derived from **κυριός** *kurios* or "Lord." The dominion is the area over which the "Lord" reigns. A similar concept in Hebrew is found where מַמְלָכָה *mamlakah* rises out of the same root as is found in kingdom, dominion, reign, royal, rule, and sovereignty. The idea is that God is the absolute authority. He reigns and rules, and is sovereign over all. He has delegated His authority to Dominions to bring things into His order.

---

[164] Colossians 2:11-15

One of the main underlying messages of redemption is that we are being invited (and empowered) to share in His victory and in extension of the Kingdom. Our original mandate in the Garden was:

> "Be fruitful and multiply; fill the earth and subdue it; have dominion over the fish of the sea, over the birds of the air, and over every living thing that moves on the earth."[165]

Being fruitful and multiplying means much more than just having children. It has to do with a theology of harvest. Before the Fall, toil "from the sweat of your brow" was not required for a harvest, just gathering it and celebrating it.[166]

Where the influence of a fallen dominion is found, one of the attendant characteristics that is all but certain to be found is rebellion. In the Kingdom, those who cooperate with the Father live in submission. The opposite of that is rebellion. It has to be excised. The seriousness of rebellion is expressed powerfully:

> For rebellion *is as* the sin of witchcraft...[167]

That shows clearly how unacceptable rebellion is to God. When He calls us to exercise dominion, there is a great restoration. Jesus calls us when he has ascended and "led captivity captive."[168] He calls us to share in the exercise of His authority and to do the very same things that He is doing. That includes not only creative things. He also wants to share His victory with us.

---

[165] Genesis 1:28
[166] Genesis 3:18
[167] 1 Samuel 15:23
[168] Psalm 68:18

Yet in all these things we are more than conquerors through Him who loved us.[169]

We should move toward victory with the same confidence we have in His resurrection. We have great inheritances that the Lord has won for us. They are both the Abundant Life and the Conquering Life. We'll talk more about that in a bit.

Virtues
On the holy side, Virtues are quite magnificent. Imagine a force of different character but like magnetism or gravity that hovers around a married couple drawing them into intimacy. Or in a time of crisis, imagine a force-field that is working to draw courage out in someone's life; God's cosmic force for good to elicit character, responsibility, truth, kindness, compassion or mercy. Virtues are like that. They are angels of urging.

Remember the old Donald Duck cartoon where a devil would be on one shoulder and an angel on the other? The red-suited, pitchfork-wielding devil would whisper temptations to Donald and the halo-in-tact angel on the other shoulder would urge him to do the "right thing." That is a caricature, of course, but it gives an idea of how Virtues work.

On God's side, Virtues urge people to be righteous and holy, and on the devil's side, they urge corruption, vice, and impurity. They both work in a similar way, but like other fallen spirits, they are not content just to try to seduce people to do the wrong thing. Since they are not satisfied with the expression of virtue, they seek to inhabit a body where they can experience the physical excesses associated with a vice. They are bent on driving their target into utter destruction, anguish, and eventually Hell. Holy Virtues are sublimely content just to do God's will. They are fulfilled when

---

[169] Romans 8:37

God is being glorified. The fallen variety can never be satisfied. That is one of the characteristics of vice.

> And at evening they return,
>> They growl like a dog,
>> And go all around the city.
> They wander up and down for food,
> And howl if they are not satisfied.[170]

Rebellion can never bring satisfaction. It has an insatiable appetite.

> He who loves silver will not be satisfied with silver;
> Nor he who loves abundance, with increase.[171]

Instead of an insatiable appetite, Godly Virtues encourage us to conform to the principles of the Kingdom and the teaching of the Scriptures. They are most content when we are in line with God's will and He is being glorified. That is where they find perfect fulfillment. We can learn from that. If we find fulfillment when God is being glorified, we will be in a place for the fruit of the Spirit to grow in our lives.

The war on the earth
For a season, God has left Satan as the "Prince of the Air," to prowl the earth. It may be hard to believe that the decision to leave him around for a season was one born of love, but it was nevertheless. His presence, however, insures that there is a great war taking place. Tragically, many people don't realize that there is a conflict at all. Speaking of his own life, a friend named Terry Moore says, "Before I found out there was a war going on, I was a P.O.W.!" That is not an uncommon experience. We found ourselves knee-deep in "dragons" even before we discovered they were real.

---

[170] Psalm 59:14-15
[171] Ecclesiastes 5:10

Strongholds

Strongholds are concentrations of spiritual strength. In the Kingdom of God, the confidence we can have in His power to save and deliver is a stronghold.

> I will love You, O LORD, my strength.
> The LORD is my rock and my fortress and my deliverer;
> My God, my strength, in whom I will trust;
> My shield and the horn of my salvation, my stronghold.[172]

But strongholds don't only stand for the Kingdom. The dark ones attempt to stand against the spread of the Gospel and the work of the Kingdom. The following is a perfect example of a stronghold.

In 2001, the House of Bishops in Uganda elected Rev. Canon David Sebuhinja to be the Bishop-elect of Muhabura Diocese. The Head of Laity and other leaders in the Diocese, however, refused to accept his appointment. This led to a five-year standoff between different groups in Muhabura Diocese and the House of Bishops.

Five years later, from 17th – 20th August 2006, Archbishop Henry Luke Orombi led a delegation of thirteen bishops from all over the Province for a weekend pastoral visit to Muhabura. The bishops went to listen to the concerns of various parties and together to seek the mind of Christ for a solution to the stalemate.

The first night in Kisoro, the Archbishop said that God woke him up in the middle of the night with the question, "Where is the pastoral staff?" In the morning,

---

[172] Psalm 18:1-2

he phoned retired Archbishop Nkoyoyo, who responded that retired Bishop Shalita had never surrendered the staff. Five years after retirement, it was still in his possession.

The Archbishop then phoned retired Bishop Shalita, who admitted that he had retired, but had not yet given up the diocese, and still had possession of the pastoral staff.

On Saturday, 19th August, retired Bishop Shalita met with the House of Bishops and delivered the pastoral staff to the Archbishop... a spiritual breakthrough.[173]

This crisis had dragged on for five years, not just because of the failure of the retired bishop to surrender his shepherd's staff as a symbol of office. It was more than that. There was a stronghold in the failure to surrender authority over the ministry in Muhabura. Notice how things quickly fell into place when the real problem was identified. It was not primarily a situation of conflict over priorities of ministry, theology, or ideas. It was instead a matter of the area being out of order. A stronghold had taken over and was not easily displaced.

Notice too, that release didn't come from "carnal weapons," but from a word of knowledge about what the true nature of the conflict was being revealed to the Archbishop.

For though we walk in the flesh, we do not war according to the flesh. 4 For the weapons of our warfare *are* not carnal but mighty in God for pulling down strongholds, 5 casting down arguments and every high

---

[173] Church of Uganda, Press Release: "Muhabura Diocese Crisis Resolved," September 7, 2006.

thing that exalts itself against the knowledge of God, bringing every thought into captivity to the obedience of Christ, <u>6</u> and being ready to punish all disobedience when your obedience is fulfilled.[174]

Notice how strongholds are arguments, and the battle against them involves "pulling them down." While God's ultimate victory is certain, this is a reminder that spiritual warfare is a struggle. Paul refers to it as a wrestling match.[175] That doesn't mean, however, that we wrestle physically. The arena is spiritual, the weapons are spiritual, and any solution that works will be born of the Spirit.

Satan's Assault
The heart of the warfare that Satan rages is terrible, though not difficult to understand in principle. There is also a common thread; always, always, always, "The thief does not come except to steal, and to kill, and to destroy."[176] Because he comes in disguise as an angel of light, he catches many unaware as he seeks to deceive us into following him into the pit.[177]

His first plan is to try to keep us from believing he is real. If he can do that, he will be able to harass us with impunity. Every chance he gets, he seeks to undermine and attack.

He is also perfectly willing to offer things that *look* good (for a time) in order to get us on the wrong path. Tragically, he doesn't even have to get us to choose things that are "evil" at first. To begin, it is enough that he just distracts us or manages to convince us that the devil doesn't exist.

---

[174] 2 Corinthians 10:3-6
[175] Ephesians 6:10
[176] John 10:10
[177] 2 Corinthians 11:14

If he can convince us that sin is not a problem, much of his work is done. People unconcerned with sin will never do much for the Kingdom. That's why Paul spends so much time in Romans 1-5 explaining the devastation that sin brings.

> For all have sinned and fallen short of the Glory of God.[178]

> The wages of sin is death.[179]

But all is not lost because God has dealt with this situation.

God took the initiative, knowing that we could not do anything ourselves to fix it.

> **8** But God demonstrates His own love toward us, in that while we were still sinners, Christ died for us. **9** Much more then, having now been justified by His blood, we shall be saved from wrath through Him. **10** For if when we were enemies we were reconciled to God through the death of His Son, much more, having been reconciled, we shall be saved by His life.[180]

The work of Jesus is sweeping. He not only overwhelms the sin that assaults an individual's life, but deals with the heart of sin itself, and He does it for the whole world.

> **11** And not only *that*, but we also rejoice in God through our Lord Jesus Christ, through whom we have now received the reconciliation.

---

[178] Romans 3:23
[179] Romans 6:23
[180] Romans 5:8-10

12 Therefore, just as through one man sin entered the world, and death through sin, and thus death spread to all men, because all sinned— **13** (For until the law sin was in the world, but sin is not imputed when there is no law. **14** Nevertheless death reigned from Adam to Moses, even over those who had not sinned according to the likeness of the transgression of Adam, who is a type of Him who was to come. **15** But the free gift *is* not like the offense. For if by the one man's offense many died, much more the grace of God and the gift by the grace of the one Man, Jesus Christ, abounded to many. **16** And the gift *is* not like *that which came* through the one who sinned. For the judgment *which came* from one *offense resulted* in condemnation, but the free gift *which came* from many offenses *resulted* in justification. **17** For if by the one man's offense death reigned through the one, much more those who receive abundance of grace and of the gift of righteousness will reign in life through the One, Jesus Christ.) **18** Therefore, as through one man's offense *judgment* came to all men, resulting in condemnation, even so through one Man's righteous act *the free gift came* to all men, resulting in justification of life. **19** For as by one man's disobedience many were made sinners, so also by one Man's obedience many will be made righteous. **20** Moreover the law entered that the offense might abound. But where sin abounded, grace abounded much more, **21** so that as sin reigned in death, even so grace might reign through righteousness to eternal life through Jesus Christ our Lord.[181]

Jesus' sacrifice powerfully provides the answer and ministry to deal with sin. From a theological standpoint, it is not only gracious, powerful and loving; it is also brilliant.

---

[181] Romans 8:5-21

Because God lives outside of time, he is not bound by time as we are. We live in the present, remember the past (partially), and wonder about the future. For Him, it is different. The past, present, and future are all alike. Imagine your life like a Monopoly board, where the present is your current place on the game board and your past is a memory. You may have tokens of remembrance of your past (deeds to properties you have purchased), but the future is entirely unknown.

For God, every day in time (past, present, and future) is present to him as concrete reality (even more than the present is to us). The terrible part of that is that any sin, no matter how long ago committed, is present to Him forever. The only way it can go anywhere, is for it to disappear into the black hole of His own death—and that is precisely what He provides for us. Beyond just being forgiven, we are given the power to change. The fruit of victorious life is not an event, but it is a process that brings us into abundant living.

Chapter Thirteen

Three Facets

Power
Glory
Forever and Ever

For Thine is the Kingdom and the Power and the Glory for ever and ever, Amen.

In this phrase of the Lord's Prayer, we commend our prayers to Him and commit to His Kingdom. We seek to see His glory multiplied. And here we see what it was all "for." It was and is for His glory. It is for His honor. It is all for Him. It was not for us. We are called to live for an audience of One, not caring what the world has to say, as long as the Holy One is pleased and honored.

I haven't always been hungry for the Kingdom in the ways that this book speaks about. For a long time, even though I was redeemed, many of my expectations were still asleep. Conversations and observations reveal I'm not the only one. Some people live with their expectations in such deep slumber that they believe they are without hope. Jesus came into a situation like that with Jairus' daughter. Jairus came to Jesus because his daughter lay at the point of death.

> And behold, one of the rulers of the synagogue came, Jairus by name. And when he saw Him, he fell at His feet 23 and begged Him earnestly, saying, "My little daughter lies at the point of death. Come and lay Your hands on her, that she may be healed, and she will live." 24 So *Jesus* went with him, and a great multitude followed Him and thronged Him.[182]

---

[182] Mark 5:22-24

Along the way, the account of Jesus healing a woman with a chronic issue of blood is delightful. The implicit messages are that not a moment is wasted and that the Kingdom flows out from Jesus, even unintentionally. It should from us, as well. Imagine what would happen if it did!

When He arrives at Jairus' house, He says,

> "Why make this commotion and weep? The child is not dead, but sleeping."[183]

Jesus shows His heart (not to mention His power) when He speaks to the girl and heals her.

> And they ridiculed Him. But when He had put them all outside, He took the father and the mother of the child, and those *who were* with Him, and entered where the child was lying. 41 Then He took the child by the hand, and said to her, "Talitha, cumi," which is translated, "Little girl, I say to you, arise." 42 Immediately the girl arose and walked, for she was twelve years *of age.* And they were overcome with great amazement.[184]

In many places today, people—even "churched" people—live in doldrums. They live pretty much without hope. This is especially true in the mainline churches that have become paralyzed by compromise, lack of purpose, and unbelief. Rather than being "the Bride of Christ," many churches look more like an emaciated girl lying on her sickbed at the point of death. They wait like sleeping beauty for the kiss of the Prince. What they don't know is that He is

---

[183] Mark 5:39
[184] Mark 5:40-42

longing for an invitation to come and kiss the Kingdom to life in us and for us.

The Power

Power in the Kingdom is very different from power in politics or nature; different even from military might. The first difference is its scale. Earthly power, in whatever form, is finite. God's power is infinite. That means He is incapable of getting tired. In Genesis, after creation, when the Scripture says "He rested,"[185] it means that he ceased creating new things. He celebrated. It doesn't mean that He was tired.

Once on a family trip to the Bahamas, I was a bit farther out in the water than my children and was facing the shore to keep an eye on them. Even though I was some distance from the shore, I was still able to stand on the bottom with my head above the water even with the little wavelets that were moving past me toward the shore. All of the sudden, I sensed something looming behind me and turned to see a huge wave, five or six feet over my head. Although I was a little startled, I wasn't afraid. My family had often vacationed at the beach and I knew to just dive into the wave. I'd done it many times and even though this wave was bigger than the ones I'd faced before, I always came out the other side without incident; so I dove through the wave.

This wave was different from any other I had ever encountered. Instead of slipping through it and popping out the other side, the cataracts of water pressed me to the sea floor. I was completely flattened and unable to move at all. There, being pressed and pressed into the sand on the bottom I tried and tried, but simply could not move at all. I suppose the "appropriate" thing to be thinking about was escape or eternity, but a very strange thought came to mind. As I lay there flattened out with tons of water rolling

---

[185] Genesis 1:2-3

over me I had a vivid memory of a bumper-sticker I had seen on the interstate highway I-35E in Dallas. It read:

> **When I die, I'll laugh at God and spit in the Devil's eye.**

My next thought was for the guy who put that sticker on his car. "He doesn't have any idea of the power he is dealing with," I thought. Here I was, one person on the sea floor. I was one person out of billions on the planet and inhabiting only one of the planets that stretched across the universe. I was overwhelmed and it didn't even take the little finger of God to do it. He who can call things that are not (yet) into being or make things to exist no more had His "hand" on my life and I couldn't negotiate, manipulate, or even move. I was totally at His mercy. It was the greatest power I had ever encountered and it was hardly a showing of His power at all. This experience made it very clear that He had the power to do whatever He chooses to do. Our prayers and our requests need to line up with His will. Then there is power aplenty to accomplish what He wants. His power will never be found lacking.

There is another aspect of godly power. It is strength "held in reserve," sometimes called meekness. Meekness isn't weakness. It is having the power at hand and choosing through discipline not to use it so that other purposes can be served. It can be as simple as holding a butterfly in your hand without crushing it. It can also be a matter of timing so someone new to the things of God has the opportunity to step out and get involved. Holding back power can also be one of the factors in allowing a spiritual solution to come to life. Clearly, Jesus held back. This powerful reality is simply expressed by Loretta Lynn in her song "Ten Thousand Angels":

> He could have called ten thousand angels to
> destroy the world and set him free

He could have called ten thousand angels but
he died alone for you and me.[186]

Jesus certainly could have manifested great power and declared victory. Instead, He chose to serve in a humiliating way. The fruit of His faithfulness is much greater by dying than it would have been if He had overthrown the angels. Indeed, it would have been a passing victory, but the price would have been tremendous. It is all too painful to admit the possibility that if He had exercised His power to fight back and overthrow those who were crucifying Him, the real battle for our salvation would have been forfeited. He would have been shown to be holy and strong. We would not have been forgiven; we would have remained unchanged and without hope.

God shares His power with us in two very different ways. He gives us the *power* to do things. This kind of power is called δυνιμισ *dynamis*. It means authority. A policeman has "the power" (authority) to tell you to stop your car. If you are a big person or have a big car, I may not have the *strength* to stop you. That kind of power is called δυνιμισ *dunimis*. It is the root word from which we get words like *dynamo, dynamic, and dynamite*. Wisdom to follow God's plan and hold back from manifesting power to know and fulfill God's will should bring supernatural results of the highest order.

Power to Create
Theologians say that creation was *ex nihilo*. They mean that God created "out of nothing." He didn't go down to the lumber yard and get the raw materials for creation. He spoke them into being. Before He spoke, nothing that we now see existed. This is a staggering power. We taste something of this creative power when

---

[186] Loretta Lynn, "Ten Thousand Angels," *Who says God is dead!*, King Records 1968.

we have children. He also allows us to participate in the release of creative power by letting us create artwork and symphonies.

Power to Keep

Another area where God demonstrates His power is in helping us with sustaining power. He keeps us and He keeps his promises. He keeps our families and He helps us keep going. It doesn't take too long walking with Him to realize our utter dependence on Him. He also works to keep the Scriptures. When you think of the miracles involved in preserving the scriptures it is absolutely staggering. Imagine what it took to keep all the various manuscripts that make up the Bible from being destroyed. An unseen hand looks to be gathering, keeping, and highlighting the Scriptures.

The Power to Transform

Eddie was a drunk. He was tough and he was mean. One night after a heavier than usual bout with a bottle, he drove to an enemy's house to teach him a lesson. From his car in the street Eddie sprayed bullets across the front of the other man's house. When he drove away, he didn't even know that his bullets had cut down the man who was standing in the dark in his own living room.

Eddie was sent to prison and spent years there. When he got out, he may have "paid his debt to society" but he was still hard and he was still mean. He was ready to get into a fist fight at the drop of a hat. Through a strange series of "coincidences" Eddie wound up visiting my parish. The Scripture lessons that day were from Ezekiel. He came up to me at the close of the service and said, "God touched me. When you read that Bible passage about how He can touch our heart and change it from a heart of stone to a heart of flesh, that's exactly what He did.[187] I don't know how He did it, but

---

[187] Ezekiel 36:26

He reached inside my chest and gave me a new heart. I'm a different man with a different heart."

This may be God's most magnificent power of all; the power to bring transformation to the human heart. What is truly amazing is that our power to sin can never match His ability to redeem, transform, and heal.

> He breaks the pow'r of cancelled sins,
> And sets the prisoner free;
> His blood can make the vilest clean,
> His blood availed for me.[188]

And The Glory
There is an old saying that says, "a lot can be accomplished if you don't care who gets the credit."[189] For us, as subjects of The King, it is a little different. Faithful servants will insist that it is the King of Kings that must get the glory. It is His right, His due; and the Kingdom is extended when we cast our crowns at His feet. He is the one who deserves the glory and acclaim. It's not that He *needs* it in order to have some sense of fulfillment. But in the environment of heaven when God gets His due, it is righteous.

For ever and ever
I flew one time to Bujumbura, Burundi on an old German plane with a stiff, awkward seat. The whole time I had to sit on a spring that stuck out of the old, flat, worn cushion. Next to me there were (no kidding) crates of live chickens lashed to the floor. Because of the economic sanctions that were in place, every day the pilot had

---

[188] Charles Wesley (1707-1788). "O for a Thousand Tongues to Sing" (1739).
[189] Shreeve, William, Ed., *Journal of the College and University Personnel Association*, v37 n3 p20-22 Fall 1986

to file a flight plan for Bukavu, Congo and then in-flight discover "a problem" that required diverting to Burundi. (The problem, of course, was a plane load of passengers that didn't want to go to Bukavu!) The flight was actually pretty short but it was bumpy and uncomfortable. Live chickens, you may know, are aromatic, but not pleasantly so. It seemed like the flight was going to last forever.

Eternity, however, doesn't just *seem* like it is going to last forever; it actually does. Even more complicated, though, is that there is more than one face of eternity. The first describes things that have a beginning, but no end. When we are redeemed, we fall into that category. Though God knew us before we were formed in the womb, there was a point in time when we were created. Once we are in Christ, however, we will have no end. We will share eternity.

God, on the other hand, has no beginning and no end. He is divinely eternal.

There is a third perspective that includes beings like the devil. From our perspective it may seem that he reaches so far back in time it seems eternal, but not being divine, he cannot actually be eternal in the past. He was created and had a beginning, but it was just before the earth. What is different about him, though, is that he will have an end. Though the devil and his agenda were defeated on the cross, the time will come when Jesus will crush the devil's head and he will be no more.[190]

For us, when we enter into eternal bliss, there will be no more tears, struggles, or pain. We will just be with the Lord and those we love. It will go on forever.

---

[190] Genesis 3:15, Mark 3:26

Section 3

Chapter Fourteen
Three Provisions

His Words
His Body and Blood
Anamnesis

"His Words"

Even before the Council of Nicea codified the Holy Scriptures, |
there were worship liturgies circulating. Probably the earliest
references are found in the writings of Clement of Rome (d. 101
AD), who referred to the celebration of the Lord's Supper
according to the words and command of Jesus. From the first
centuries of the life of the church, the Eucharist, or Lord's Supper,
followed the same pattern that Jesus used (see the previous section
on Taken, Blessed, Broken, Given). The minimal "formula" usually
included four items:

a. A prayer to gather the people (*Sursum cordia*- Latin: "Lift
   up your hearts."), usually including confession of sins.
b. Scripture reading always including a Gospel reading.
c. The "Manual Acts" of Jesus (Taken, Blessed, etc.).
d. "His Words" (i.e., "This is My Body, This is My
   Blood...").

Because the Lord's Supper was a direct command of Jesus and
included the words that He used, communion has always had a
central place in Christian worship. Paul speaks of it as a central
teaching.

> For I received from the Lord that which I also delivered
> to you: that the Lord Jesus on the *same* night in which He
> was betrayed took bread; <u>24</u> and when He had given
> thanks, He broke *it* and said, "Take, eat; this is My body

229

which is broken for you; do this in remembrance of Me."
25 In the same manner *He* also *took* the cup after supper, saying, "This cup is the new covenant in My blood. This do, as often as you drink *it,* in remembrance of Me."
26 For as often as you eat this bread and drink this cup, you proclaim the Lord's death till He comes.
27 Therefore whoever eats this bread or drinks *this* cup of the Lord in an unworthy manner will be guilty of the body and blood of the Lord. 28 But let a man examine himself, and so let him eat of the bread and drink of the cup. 29 For he who eats and drinks in an unworthy manner eats and drinks judgment to himself, not discerning the Lord's body. 30 For this reason many *are* weak and sick among you, and many sleep.[191]

Notice that sickness and even death (sleep) are attributed to eating and drinking the elements of communion in an unworthy manner. Many churches today that have not historically come out of the sacramental tradition are discovering the great supernatural power in receiving communion according to the theology of "His Words."

His Body and His Blood
Many evangelicals have seen communion as a memorial of what Jesus did. Those from the sacramental perspective see it as much more. These days, there is a wave of discovery among evangelicals, charismatics, and Pentecostals seeing the supernatural dimension of both baptism and communion. It is less important to nail down *how* it happens than to recognize *that* it does. Rightly celebrated, communion offers us the same power, grace, victory, forgiveness, and freedom that would come from us receiving the Body and Blood of the freshly resurrected Jesus of Galilee. In receiving the elements of communion, we should expect to be healed and delivered, encouraged and nurtured, reconciled and challenged.

---

[191] 1 Corinthians 11:23-30

The prayer, "Let these elements be for us the Body and Blood of Your Son according to Your promise," is one that resonates into the heart of heaven. The power that is resident stretches beyond the limits of our imagination.

Do this in Remembrance—Anamnesis "The anamnesis states who is remembered (Jesus) and what is done in remembrance (the bread is broken and the cup is shared)."[192] Anamnesis is the concept of doing something in time here and now that is supernaturally linked to an event (or events) in the past. Theologians talk about this as things "standing outside time."

The chief example of something that stands outside time is the Cross itself. Jesus doesn't have to die each week for the sins of that week. The one sacrifice He offered two thousand years ago "works" as the remedy for our sins today, those yet uncommitted and those of yesterday that we have forgotten. Anamnesis describes the bridge between that which is possible in the mind of God and what we experience here and now. Of course, we are honoring what Jesus did, but the glory of His sacrifice is multiplied when it is recognized and applied in our lives today.

---

[192] St. James Presbyterian Church *Celebrating, Communion, Confirmation Resources, The Nuts and Bolts of Our Faith*, Unit 7. (Chicago, Illinois 2007)

Chapter Fifteen
Three Obligations

Serve His Purpose/Plan
Serve His Way
Serve His Timetable

Prayer in His Name
Most prayers by Christians end "in Jesus' name." It may *seem* more
powerful when prayed with a polysyllabic emphasis: "in Juh-eee-
sus name," but the real power is in praying His plan and His will.
Sadly, I can't remember ever hearing a sermon with emphasis put
into figuring out *why* we pray in His name. Too often, it seems like
it is some sort of celestial zip code that is added on to insure
heavenly delivery. That, however, is not what is meant by "praying
in the name of Jesus."

Probably the best model to describe prayer in the name of Jesus
comes from a legal document called *Power of Attorney*. Power of
Attorney is an authorization for one person to represent *the interests*
of another, according to the limits of the document. For example, a
Medical Power of Attorney gives a person the authority to
represent the one who has granted the document in terms of
medical care. It can also be prepared to allow legal representation
across a range of issues.

There is a special kind of intercession that has been given to us
when we pray "in His name." To call God's best to life in the lives
of people that we pray for, we can pray and ask God to show us
what it is in their life that He wants to see developed in them. If
you think of that image as a slide, we can pray so that the light of
Christ shines through them and the image of the way God sees
them in their potential is projected into the future. We can call that
image to life in them. It can be healing, wholeness, fulfillment of

potential, or the development of gifts. As we participate in God's vision for their life and call them to it, they can't help but be blessed.

> In order to be effective, the content of our prayers needs to be what God desires.[193]

Prayer and Dominion
When God created us it was with nobility in mind. God chose to share dominion with mankind. He didn't have to, He chose to. When sin entered the garden and polluted our lives, it was a terrible blow. It brought death and separation. But never forget that you were created for greatness. When our life in Christ comes alive, we are called back to our original mandate and purpose. And that is to exercise dominion over creation.

> 3 When I consider Your heavens, the work of Your fingers,
>> The moon and the stars, which You have ordained,
> 4 What is man that You are mindful of him,
>> And the son of man that You visit him?
> 5 For You have made him a little lower than the angels,
>> And You have crowned him with glory and honor.
> 6 You have made him to have dominion over the works of Your hands;
>> You have put all *things* under his feet,
> 7 All sheep and oxen—
>> Even the beasts of the field,
> 8 The birds of the air,
>> And the fish of the sea

---

[193] Sheets. *Authority in Prayer.* Op cit. Page 106

In the case of Jesus, He has given us authority to represent Him. |
He has delegated dominion, the extension of the Kingdom, and
even signs and wonders to us. But He expects us to seek His
timing, methods, and will before acting. We need to ask because
the world is far more complex than it first appears. We are treading
on thin ice, presuming we understand everything we need to know
in order to act.

There is a great deal of confusion (and no small manner of anguish)
when people *assume* that they know God's will and timing. This
does not mean that we need to pray with a lack of faith. God
certainly has the power to act miraculously and supernaturally. He
is the creator of the universe and is hardly stymied by the
challenges our lives present. He is always loving. The question is
whether or not we, who "see through a glass darkly," are acting on
His timetable or in accordance with His plan. We know,
uncontrovertibly, that He is good. We know with confidence that
He is able and we should press in to Him to ask Him to act. We
may not know why things don't turn out as we ask sometimes, but
that should not stop us from asking. |

Praying with Confidence, *not* Arrogance
Who are you? Can you answer that with confidence? Are you
married? Are you a citizen of Switzerland? Are you American,
English, or Ugandan? Are you right or left handed? Do you like
brussel sprouts? By the way, for those who are interested, brussel
sprouts are *brassica oleracea var gemmifera* (I know you are thankful
to get *that* covered!). To a farmer they are a cash crop. To most kids,
they are just plain "yuk," but whatever the opinion, *everyone* knows
confidently how they stand on the brussel sprout issue.

---

[194] Psalm 8:3-8

Whatever shades there may be to those questions, those are not the sorts of things that are confusing to answer. When it comes to spiritual things, however, many people seem to waffle terribly. With the rise of postmodernism, relativism has strongly taken root. Because the Christian faith is based on truth revealed by God, we should be able to have confidence in what He has revealed. We don't need to know *everything* about the Kingdom to be able to speak with confidence about the things we *do* know.

Think of it like a city. You probably don't know every street, shop, and corner like a London cabbie, but you do know some parts of it. You know the street where you live. The place you work. Where you worship. But it is not dishonest to say that you "know" your hometown, even if your knowledge is incomplete.

You are called to preach, teach, and share what you know of the Kingdom. You are called to manifest its power and declare its truth. And you are called to do so with power.

> ...that we who first trusted in Christ should be to the praise of His glory. 13 In Him you also *trusted,* after you heard the word of truth, the gospel of your salvation; in whom also, having believed, you were sealed with the Holy Spirit of promise, 14 who is the guarantee of our inheritance until the redemption of the purchased possession, to the praise of His glory.[195]

We are to *be* to the praise of His Glory. That means we are to live, work, and yearn for His glory to be manifest; for His Kingdom to be manifest in a way that honors God. Because we have been sealed by the Holy Spirit, we can proceed with confidence.

---

[195] Ephesians 1:12-14

Confidence is conviction regarding something that is known to be true. But that does not mean that arrogance is acceptable. Arrogance is presumption to claim more than we should.

> "Talk no more so very proudly;
>> Let no arrogance come from your mouth,
>> For the LORD *is* the God of knowledge;
>> And by Him actions are weighed.[196]

It is not arrogance to say that I am married. It is not arrogance to say that it is Christ's nature to heal. When I speak qualitatively about a situation, however, I am on much more shaky ground. To say, "I am a *better* American than so-and-so," or "I am a *better* Christian," is arrogant.

Confidence in intercession is to be desired. To know that God *can* move, heal, and deliver is a position of strength. But we are to pray for revelation from Him concerning *how and when* He will move. To *presume* is to sin no matter how reasonable the presumption seems to us.

In the fifth century, St. Augustine said, "True humility is the ability to make an accurate appraisal of yourself."[197]

Coming into the knowledge of our sin is crucially important so we can be rid of it. We may fear rejection from other Christians, leaders, or even God Himself, but rejection is not the fruit of honesty; it is, however, repentance.

---

[196] 1 Samuel 1:28

[197] Albert C. Outler, Ph.D., D.D., *Introduction and Translation of Confessions of St. Augustine*, Perkins School of Theology, Dallas, 1955.

The abbot Pastor [Pastor was his name] said, 'If a man has sinned and denies it not, but says, 'I have sinned,' scold him not, for thou wilt break the purpose of his heart. But rather say to him, 'Be not sad, my brother, but watch thyself hereafter,' and thou wilt rouse his heart to repentance.'[198]

If I know myself before God, I will come to Him with the knowledge of my frailties, but with utter confidence in Him and His ability to act. The problem is that "we see through a glass darkly."[199] But that is not all there is. We also have the promise that "we shall see face to face."[200] We can ask for more knowledge. We can seek His will and His face. We can see Him move more than we have, but we should also be honest that there are some things we don't yet know or understand. In a wonderful way, honesty about whatever shortfall there may be doesn't detract from our credibility; it actually confirms it.

And so we pray with confidence, not arrogance. Jesus has opened access to God for us. We can approach God boldly, but should never forget that He is the One in charge. He is the One who is the Lord and He is the One who decides what needs to be done. Our job is to listen, follow, and obey.

One church I know takes listening and intercessory prayer so seriously that when they have times for healing prayer, they have a team of intercessors who gather in the next room to pray for those who are praying for healing! You can well imagine how much that

---

[198] Helen Waddell, *The Desert Fathers–Book Ten: Of Discretion, XLIV*, (Ann Arbor: University of Michigan Press, 1957.) Page 103.
[199] 1 Corinthians 13:12
[200] Ibid. 1 Corinthians 13:12

improves our ability to hear and what a wonderful experience it is for those who receive prayer!

Chapter Sixteen
Three Venues

The Family
The Gathered Body
Marketplace

The Family
Many wonderful resources have been written about Christian family life, so I'm not going to attempt to re-cover the field in depth. Instead, there are a few issues about family that bear highlighting in relation to the Kingdom.

Unity
At the heart of the family is marriage. It is a wonderful picture of the unity found in God Himself and it also provides a picture of relationship between Jesus and His Bride.

> The bond and covenant of marriage was established by God in creation, and our Lord Jesus Christ adorned this manner of life by his presence and first miracle at a wedding in Cana of Galilee. It signifies to us the mystery of the union between Christ and his Church, and Holy Scripture commends it to be honored among all people.[201]

Unity provides a tremendous vantage point. It is like the difference between beginning to swim and being able to push off the side of a pool. Spiritually, the impact of agreement can be seen in a tremendous increase of effectiveness.

How could one chase a thousand,

---

[201] Book of Common Prayer, "Celebration and Blessing of Marriage," page 423.

And two put ten thousand to flight?[202]

Sadly, far too few married couples take advantage of the power that is available to them in praying prayers of agreement. My wife and I have come into a real appreciation of the power that our unified prayers have, especially in dealing with family concerns. It is sad that we spend so many years missing the mark. Now, we take the time to discuss, listen, and ask the Holy Spirit to guide us so we can be in full agreement when we pray every day. It is far more than a "coincidence" that we see much more fruit from our prayers of agreement.

The Christian family is also the first place that the Body of Christ is manifest. Children are exposed to the incarnation of Christ's love and they see the order of heaven displayed in godly parents. It is the perfect venue for evangelism even though it is challenging. I can't think of any other place where hypocrisy is more readily unmasked! A dear friend who is an Anglican Archbishop was invited to speak to a large gathering of Roman Catholic Bishops. In the question and answer period, one of the things the Roman Bishops asked was, "What do you have as an Anglican Bishop that we as Roman Catholics don't have?"

After thinking for a moment my friend replied, "I have a wife and children who are willing to say to me, 'Oh, Dad, don't be so stupid!'" While St. Paul opined that being married offered complications that were not present in the single life, there is also a great strength that comes from marriage and family. While a vocation to singleness is not to be diminished in any way, there is a great synergy that comes as we are multiplied through our spouses and children.

Complementariness

---

[202] Deuteronomy 32:29

That is a rather awkward word to describe how a husband and wife complete each other. What is so wonderfully figured in a physical way is also demonstrated in the way that men and women are so delightfully different and yet can come together so magnificently in marriage. It is also evident in the very different ways that men and women process information and make decisions. One is not better than the other, they are just as different as the way that men and women use a TV remote! Men "fire" the remote to "hunt" for a channel; women nurture it to coax information out of the set.

The Gathered Body

> "Again I say to you that if two of you agree on earth concerning anything that they ask, it will be done for them by My Father in heaven. 20 For where two or three are gathered together in My name, I am there in the midst of them."[203]

To ask for something "in Jesus name" is discussed in the section on prayer, but suffice it to say here, that Jesus is not giving license for everyone to have a lake house and an airplane. The key message here is that Jesus is in the midst when we gather in His name.

While there are some tremendous advantages to being part of a large church, God is present in tiny gatherings as well. When the meeting of the gathered body is a small group, the idea is to build relationships, minister to people, and help them discover gifts that can be deployed in ministry as they reach out. Small groups are the perfect environment for helping people to be healed and transformed.[204] When the gathering is a large one, it is well suited to worship and vision casting. There is also a dynamic that rises from large gatherings of believers where faith is released and

---

[203] Matthew 18:19f
[204] Acts 20:20

wonderful miracles seem easier to come by. Contemporary music worship styles are dramatically easier when there are more than three hundred and fifty people, but meaningful worship can take place with far fewer. It takes focus and openness. In the absence of a skilled worship leader/musician, recorded music can be used for small groups.

The Marketplace

In the 16th century, the Reformation restored the Scriptures to the people. It was fueled by the convergence of four things. First, Reformers like Martin Luther were graced with a rediscovery of the Gospel of grace and the truth of the revelation of the authority of the Scriptures. Second, the Holy Spirit was moving, yearning, and longing in much the same way He did in creation for this fire to come to life. The third influence was the spiritual corruption of the Roman Catholic Church that was selling indulgences. Indulgences were the quintessential example of bad doctrine where people paid money into the church coffers in order for the church to declare that their sins were forgiven. The fourth factor was the invention of the movable type printing press.

While all these things were important, it is fascinating that the one that released the Scriptures to mass distribution was something that happened in the marketplace. Gutenberg's printing press was a commercial invention that was focused on printing Bibles. Of course, it was also used for many other printing jobs, but its most noble application was getting the Word of God to the masses. Many other inventions and technological advancements are just waiting to be discovered that will have just as great an impact as the printing press did.

There is another revolution/reformation taking place today. It was pre-figured over the last thirty years with the rediscovery of the ministry of the people of God. The last several decades generated a lot of excitement about "lay ministry." The idea that church members should share in the ministry of the church is a powerful one and paved the way for some strong and extremely active congregations to develop. Lay ministry, however, was just the prelude to the real revolution/reformation. It is the release of Christian mission and ministry in and through the marketplace.

Ezekiel prophesied about water (a figure of life and ministry) proceeding from the altar and going out across the city and across the world. Unlike most springs of water in the desert, the farther away Ezekiel moved from the source, the deeper the water got.

> 1 Then he brought me back to the door of the temple; and there was water, flowing from under the threshold of the temple toward the east, for the front of the temple faced east; the water was flowing from under the right side of the temple, south of the altar. 2 He brought me out by way of the north gate, and led me around on the outside to the outer gateway that faces east; and there was water, running out on the right side.
> 3 And when the man went out to the east with the line in his hand, he measured one thousand cubits, and he brought me through the waters; the water *came up to my* ankles. 4 Again he measured one thousand and brought me through the waters; the water *came up to my* knees. Again he measured one thousand and brought me through; the water *came up to my* waist. 5 Again he measured one thousand, *and it was* a river that I could not cross; for the water was too deep, water in which one must swim, a river that could not be crossed. 6 He said to me, "Son of man, have you seen *this?*" Then he brought me and returned me to the bank of the river.[205]

---

[205] Ezekiel 47:1-6

This prophetic vision runs counter to the normal way that water works. It is a powerful picture of how the world is impacted when ministry is no longer centered around the church, but people are transformed in order to be agents of transformation. The only way that is going to happen on such a grand scale is when ministry returns to the marketplace.

For several generations, the role of Christians in business has been thought to be a commission to make a lot of money so they can give it to the church. Many Christian business people have been inspirationally faithful in doing that. In addition, to be a Christian in business has meant witnessing to people as the opportunity presented itself. That will continue to be true, since it is true for all of us, everywhere, all the time.

Marketplace ministry, however, is a different way of looking at things. It involves discipling, encouraging, and releasing people to enter business as points of mission, ministry, and transformation. Marketplace companies use their business model to impact lives. It is not just that the Gospel is shared on coffee breaks and lunch hours, the whole endeavor is set up to transform lives—everything about the business is set up to serve that purpose. Goods and services are designed to extend the Kingdom to customers. But the Kingdom business will do more than that. There is a commitment to minister to employees' lives and families. Many companies have discovered the value of having paid chaplains to facilitate discipleship and care for workers and their families. A few avant garde firms even have paid intercessors who come in to work every day to pray for the people who work there, the needs in employee families, and for the Holy Spirit to shape business deals to line up with God's will. Most amazing is the concept of praying for competitors as well! If we take the Gospel seriously, that is what *normal* Kingdom businesses will look like.

It is obvious that we have a long way to go to get this released. There have been huge roadblocks, however. Most churches haven't even been able to get the church members released into meaningful ministry. In far too many congregations, a church member in the hospital who is not visited by the Senior Pastor will feel like the church abandoned them no matter how many other people came, cared, prayed, and provided for them.

It is not just a focus on the pastor though that is a problem. There is an artificial distinction between things that are considered holy and things that are worldly or profane. The false dichotomy of secular and sacred has allowed people to polish themselves up on Sunday morning and then live like Hell during the week. Clearly, that is *not* God's design.

Imagine instead a model of Christian life where ministry and everyday life overlap. Not just because we are out giving our testimony during the workday, but because the Kingdom is integrally woven into our lives, so it surfaces naturally.

We recently had a problem with our two year old air conditioning system (a necessity in Texas where temperatures often rise over 100 degrees in the summer). A series of botched service calls and communications difficulties resulted in a high quality unit being taken out unnecessarily, a cheap brand being installed improperly, and the capacity being degraded and inadequate. When I went through the litany of problems with the two companies involved, one washed their hands of the problem and said that they had no responsibility, even though their mistake had led to the unit being removed. The manager of the other company sat with me and then said, "Let me work on this. We want to make everything right. I live in this town. I have grandchildren here. I go to church here. I want to make it right."

Over a period of weeks, he negotiated the removal of all the inferior equipment and arranged with a top level manufacturer to take everything back and install the larger high efficiency unit that was called for from the start. They offered to do all of this for just the difference of cost, had the proper unit been originally installed two years ago. They were committed to what we needed and what was right. What a tremendous witness from a righteous man. Now, if he were to come to me and say, "Let me tell you the difference a relationship with Jesus Christ can make," I'd be constrained to listen. And that is precisely what is happening in Kingdom businesses that are cropping up all over the world.

Notice how the impact of ministry not only increases in depth as the water (spirit-life and ministry) flows from the temple. Notice how it flows down the valley to the Dead Sea and brings it to life.

> When I returned, there, along the bank of the river, *were* very many trees on one side and the other. 8 Then he said to me: "This water flows toward the eastern region, goes down into the valley, and enters the sea. *When it* reaches the sea, *its* waters are healed. 9 And it shall be *that* every living thing that moves, wherever the rivers go, will live. There will be a very great multitude of fish, because these waters go there; for they will be healed, and everything will live wherever the river goes. 10 It shall be *that* fishermen will stand by it from En Gedi to En Eglaim; they will be *places* for spreading their nets. Their fish will be of the same kinds as the fish of the Great Sea, exceedingly many. 11 But its swamps and marshes will not be healed; they will be given over to salt. 12 Along the bank of the river, on this side and that, will grow all *kinds of* trees used for food; their leaves will not wither, and their fruit will not fail. They will bear fruit every month, because their water flows from the sanctuary.

Their fruit will be for food, and their leaves for medicine."[206]

When marketplace ministry is released, it brings life and freedom. What is fascinating about this prophetic passage is that it may well be literally true as well as figuratively. There is a plan afoot to flood fresh water on top of the Dead Sea. Fresh water is lighter and will float. The difference of salt and fresh water provides several things. First of all, there is a temperature differential between the fresh and salt water that can be exploited to drive turbines to produce electricity. In this case, two feet of fresh water on top of the Dead Sea would provide enough energy from temperature differential to drive turbines that could provide electricity for the entire Middle East! In addition, the virtually lifeless Dead Sea would, with just a few feet of fresh water topping, be able to sustain vast quantities of aquatic life for commercial fishing. Isn't God's Word amazing!

---

[206] Ezekiel 47:7-12

Chapter Seventeen

Three Commands

Love!
- God
- Neighbor
- One another

Go!
- Make disciples of nations
- As the Father sent Me, I send you
- Go preach the Kingdom

Seek!
- … the lost sheep
- … and you will find
- First the Kingdom

Love

The nature, character, and actions of God epitomize love. He is the essence of love and always acts in loving ways. Overwhelmingly, He has demonstrated His love for us in that "while we were yet sinners, Christ died for us."[207]

That action on His part completely redefines everything. It also demands a response. It just isn't reasonable to come to know that we are loved in that way and fail to have it revolutionize the way we live.

Loving God

No matter how difficult His actions may be to understand, God's every action and every purpose is filled with love. That's a warm and fuzzy idea, but there is a difficult side to it as well. It is hard for boundary-fuzzed postmodern people to accept that love might

---

[207] Romans 5:8

result in pain. That would never have been an issue in previous generations who realized that it is a "fearful thing to fall into the hands of the living God."[208] God has been very clear that following Him is not a rose garden. It is a painful course, but it is not pain without hope.

> "If anyone desires to come after Me, let him deny himself, and take up his cross, and follow Me. <u>25</u> For whoever desires to save his life will lose it, but whoever loses his life for My sake will find it.[209]

He also promises:

> In the world you will have tribulation; but be of good cheer, I have overcome the world."[210]

One of the earliest things to which we are called by God is found in Deuteronomy:

> "Hear, O Israel: The LORD our God, the LORD *is* one! <u>5</u> You shall love the LORD your God with all your heart, with all your soul, and with all your strength.[211]

With all that we have, and all that we are, we are called to honor Him. If that sounds like an impossible task and an unreasonable challenge, then we must remember that we live in the light of the Cross and resurrection that has demonstrated exactly that kind of love.

---

[208] Hebrews 10:30
[209] Matthew 16:24-25
[210] John 16:33
[211] Deuteronomy 6:4

My grandmother used to make molasses drop cookies. Once you had one, you were hooked forever. The Father's love is even better!

Loving Neighbors

If we follow and emulate Him, we are called to manifest exactly the same standard of love, impossible though it may seem. Love demands that we seek God's best in people's lives and that we act in ways that produce love's fruit in their lives. Love is not a sloppy sentimentality that cheers people on in their passions, no matter how destructive. Though that is the thoughtless heartbeat of contemporary culture, it is not the way we are called by Christ to live. We are agents of love, no matter how challenging or uncomfortable that position might be. We are to love without reservation not just because we have been told to do so, but because that is the way we were first loved when we didn't deserve it. The weight of responsibility to respond to His love is huge. The fruit of doing so is promised to be magnificent.

The demands of love that are genuine and robust are penetrating. They go way beyond the "Ooo, you have spinach caught in your teeth," into relationships of substance that call us to be real.

In the wonderful children's story *The Velveteen Rabbit*, the Skin Horse tells his story to the Rabbit.

> "What is REAL?" asked the Rabbit one day, when they were lying side by side near the nursery fender, before Nana came to tidy the room. "Does it mean having things that buzz inside you and a stick-out handle?"

> "Real isn't how you are made," said the Skin Horse. "It's a thing that happens to you. When a child loves you for a long, long time, not just to play with, but REALLY loves you, then you become Real."

"Does it hurt?" asked the Rabbit.

"Sometimes," said the Skin Horse, for he was always truthful. "When you are Real you don't mind being hurt."

"Does it happen all at once, like being wound up," he asked, "or bit by bit?"

"It doesn't happen all at once," said the Skin Horse. "You become. It takes a long time. That's why it doesn't happen often to people who break easily, or have sharp edges, or who have to be carefully kept. Generally, by the time you are Real, most of your hair has been loved off, and your eyes drop out and you get loose in the joints and very shabby. But these things don't matter at all, because once you are Real you can't be ugly, except to people who don't understand."[212]

And so it is in the Kingdom as the Great Lover loves us. It is a pricey proposition, but the rewards far outweigh the cost. And so it should be for us, as well, as we become extravagant forgivers, encouragers, and lovers. We are called to *be* Jesus to people and to love them into being real. I'm not even going to try to say exactly what that looks like—there are too many facets possible. But real love keeps what is best for others in mind. Not only will that be praying for them as Jesus did, but sometimes it will mean speaking the truth to them in a very challenging way.

Love One another
There is another dimension to loving our neighbors. It is the love we are commanded to demonstrate to those in the household of faith. Love of (and for) the brethren has the added dimension that it

---

[212] Margery Williams, *The Velveteen Rabbit-How toys become real.* (Garden City, NY: Doubleday & Co., 1922.) Page 3.

is one of the chief vehicles by which the world will know that we are disciples. Sadly, the church has been a place without much of a redemptive track record when it comes to the way we treat each other. Particularly egregious is the way believers generally treat those who fall into sin. The normal model is to just shoot the wounded and give them the left foot of fellowship casting them into the darkness, but that is not the Kingdom way.

> 1 Brethren, if a man is overtaken in any trespass, you who *are* spiritual restore such a one in a spirit of gentleness, considering yourself lest you also be tempted. 2 Bear one another's burdens, and so fulfill the law of Christ. 3 For if anyone thinks himself to be something, when he is nothing, he deceives himself.[213]

There are ample opportunities to demonstrate this kind of love and restoration because there are so many times when we hurt each other. Restoring does not mean ignoring. It is like a medical restoration in which wounds are healed. Even beyond healing, however, is the Kingdom principle of *transfiguration*. That is the process by which wounds become strengths, just like they did in Jesus' life. Who can fail to be inspired by the nail prints or the rend in His side? Kingdom loving overwhelms wounds. It may take longer than we like, and it may come differently than we expect, but we have hope in Christ for healing.

Go!
The second command of the Kingdom is to *go*. There are three main ways of expression. The first is the command from Matthew 28, to "go," and it is principally expressed in three ways. The first is a command to μαθητευσατε παντα τα εθνη (*matheteusate panta ta ethne*) to "disciple all the nations."[214]

---

[213] Galatians 6:1-3
[214] Matthew 28:19

How miserably short we have fallen from that command. How easy it is to be distracted from our noble calling to get our attention diverted to leaky roofs and the demands of raising money for the budget. How many uninspiring board meetings must we endure before we fix our energy and resources on our real calling. Far too often, even in our best and most noble congregations, a few Christians have engaged the idea that we might make disciples *in* all the nations, but many churches even fall short of that. The vision of a church that brings the Gospel to bear to change the surrounding culture is hard to find. Rather than just hanging on or surviving, we are called to exercise dominion and live in a way that extends the Kingdom to impact the culture. At the end of the day, there ought to be an abundance of Kingdom fruit, the extension of the purpose for which Jesus came into the world. The landscape should be littered with those who have been healed, delivered, saved (from all manner of perils!), set free, and encouraged.

If the transformation of the culture is not the fruit of our current labors, what shall we do? Rise up! Do the work that God has given us to do. He has not left us comfortless. He has not forgotten His servants. He wants to help us bear magnificent fruit.

> "If you love Me, keep My commandments. 16 And I will pray the Father, and He will give you another Helper, that He may abide with you forever— 17 the Spirit of truth, whom the world cannot receive, because it neither sees Him nor knows Him; but you know Him, for He dwells with you and will be in you. 18 I will not leave you orphans; I will come to you.[215]

The diminution comes when we simply offer Him the opportunity to bless our "lesser stuff." Those mundane offerings are hardly the

---

[215] John 14:15-18

inspiring and noble vocation of restoration to which He has called us; neither will they bring the world to Christ.

Go! As the Father Sent Me, I send you.
While the "Great Commission" of Matthew 28 is well known, a more sweeping direction is given in John 20. After the crucifixion, the disciples locked themselves in the Banquet Room of the Jerusalem Holiday Inn. They may have originally gathered for fear of the Jews and the concern that the fate of Jesus might come to them as well. In any case, it was into that room that the risen Jesus came, breathed them to life, and commissioned them:

> Then, the same day at evening, being the first *day* of the week, when the doors were shut where the disciples were assembled, for fear of the Jews, Jesus came and stood in the midst, and said to them, "Peace *be* with you." <u>20</u> When He had said this, He showed them *His* hands and His side. Then the disciples were glad when they saw the Lord.
> <u>21</u> So Jesus said to them again, "Peace to you! As the Father has sent Me, I also send you." <u>22</u> And when He had said this, He breathed on *them,* and said to them, "Receive the Holy Spirit. <u>23</u> If you forgive the sins of any, they are forgiven them; if you retain the *sins* of any, they are retained."[216]

"As the Father has sent Me, I also send you." There you have it. We are sent with the same purpose as Jesus Himself. He was sent to heal, deliver, save, and love, and so are we. We are called to walk in the same power, love with the same limitless vision, and call people's destiny to life.

---

[216] John 20:19-23

More than challenging, that vocation is very precisely, *humanly impossible!* We have a part in the process, but it is a very limited one.

> We don't have to produce anything—reconciliation, deliverance, victory, etc.—but rather we distribute, as the disciples did with the loaves and fishes.[217]

If God does not supply the power and resources that are needed, we are more than sunk. We are pitiful. What strength resides in me that can forgive sins or set a captive free? What power do I possess that can accomplish what I am called to do? It is nothing that I possess. It is a gift lavishly given by the Giver Who seeks to share His love. Preserve me, O God, for it is in You I put my trust.

> 2 *O my soul*, you have said to the LORD,
>   "You *are* my Lord,
>   My goodness is nothing apart from You."[218]

On my own, it is overwhelming, but with His power at work in me, anything is possible.

> To this *end* I also labor, striving according to His working which works in me mightily.[219]

> "My grace is sufficient for you, for My strength is made perfect in weakness."[220]

---

[217] Sheets, *Intercessory Prayer*. page 41.
[218] Psalm 16:2
[219] Colossians 1:29
[220] 2 Corinthians 12:9

"Success" in the Kingdom does not rely on us. It relies on the work of God the Holy Spirit, but He has chosen not to work unless we cooperate.

Go preach the Kingdom
There is a great deal of evangelical momentum to "preach the Gospel," and a great deal of energy invested in trying to do that throughout the world. By that, what is usually meant is preaching that presents the saving Lordship of Jesus Christ in a joinable fashion. The goal, of course, is for people to enter into a relationship with Jesus and be saved. The Greek term for salvation is σωζω *sozo*. To be "saved," or coming into a saving relationship with Jesus Christ means much more than just inheriting eternal life (as magnificent as that is!). The meanings of the term σωζω *sozo* stretch well beyond salvation to include being rescued, lifted up from the mire, restored, forgiven, healed, and made whole. However, even with the understanding that salvation brings many more dimensions of blessing to our life with God, the message of the Kingdom is even greater. Preaching the Gospel of the Kingdom means to extend the reign of God, furthering the dominion of Christ, and sharing the healing graces of restoration. It means that this world gets to be more and more like Heaven.

When Jesus sends us out, He wants us to do more than proclaim things about the Kingdom that are true, He wants us to extend the truth of the Kingdom into more and more places and into more and more people's lives.

Seek!
The second command of the Kingdom *to seek* has three faces. The first is to **seek the lost sheep.** The first step of that was Jesus sending His disciples to the lost sheep of Israel. It's not that He isn't interested in the others, it was a matter of timing. The real key principle, however, is that Jesus has a passion for the lost. He wants

them to proactively pursue the lost sheep. Not only that, but they are to pursue them with the power and the glory of the Kingdom.

> "Do not go into the way of the Gentiles, and do not enter a city of the Samaritans. 6 But go rather to the lost sheep of the house of Israel. 7 And as you go, preach, saying, "The kingdom of heaven is at hand.' 8 Heal the sick, cleanse the lepers, raise the dead, cast out demons. Freely you have received, freely give. 9 Provide neither gold nor silver nor copper in your money belts"[221]

Salvation is to be proclaimed in an orderly fashion. First, gather those in the house of Israel who have not yet responded. To attract them (and to share the love of the Father) heal, cleanse, and set them free. Don't rely on your own resources. Leave even the (cheap) copper coins behind. They won't help with manifesting Kingdom power anyway.

Lest we think that "gathering" is a singular calling only for some disciples, Jesus shares other parables to make His intention clear.

> "What man of you, having a hundred sheep, if he loses one of them, does not leave the ninety-nine in the wilderness, and go after the one which is lost until he finds it? 5 And when he has found *it,* he lays *it* on his shoulders, rejoicing. 6 And when he comes home, he calls together *his* friends and neighbors, saying to them, "Rejoice with me, for I have found my sheep which was lost!' 7 I say to you that likewise there will be more joy in heaven over one sinner who repents than over ninety-nine just persons who need no repentance.[222]

---

[221] Matthew 10:5-9
[222] Luke 15:4-7

There is nothing in the world that has as much value as the soul of a man, woman, or child. If our hearts beat with the rhythm of the Kingdom, we will recognize that and do everything we can to reach people. If we have been ravaged by transforming grace, we live under love's burden and constraint that others, too, will come to know Him and experience the freedom that Christ can bring.

Seek and you will find
This oft quoted (and mostly misunderstood) statement by Jesus is not, in fact, the promise that every search made on our own terms will bear fruit. There is a hint in Matthew's version that searches will yield "good things."

> "Ask, and it will be given to you; seek, and you will find; knock, and it will be opened to you. 8 For everyone who asks receives, and he who seeks finds, and to him who knocks it will be opened. 9 Or what man is there among you who, if his son asks for bread, will give him a stone? 10 Or if he asks for a fish, will he give him a serpent? 11 If you then, being evil, know how to give good gifts to your children, how much more will your Father who is in heaven give good things to those who ask Him![223]

The similar passage in Luke yields the treasure of letting us know what the "good things" are that God is eager to give to us:

> "So I say to you, ask, and it will be given to you; seek, and you will find; knock, and it will be opened to you. 10 For everyone who asks receives, and he who seeks finds, and to him who knocks it will be opened. 11 If a son asks for bread from any father among you, will he give him a stone? Or if *he asks* for a fish, will he give him a serpent instead of a fish? 12 Or if he asks for an egg, will he offer

---

[223] Matthew 7:7-11

him a scorpion? <u>13</u> If you then, being evil, know how to give good gifts to your children, how much more will *your* heavenly Father give *the Holy Spirit* to those who ask Him!"[224]

While many good things come to us from the Father, the premiere "good thing" that the Father promises to give is the Holy Spirit. There may be other treasures that are discovered or other gifts that are found, but the best of all is the Holy Spirit. In giving Him to us, we have the life and love of God manifest in our hearts. Nothing else can compare with that.

The third face of this command is that we *seek first the Kingdom.* It is a commandment that comes with a promise.

> <u>33</u> But seek first the kingdom of God and His righteousness, and all these things shall be added to you.[225]

That is an incredibly bold promise! If we seek the Kingdom first, every desire of our heart will be fulfilled. How can God make that promise? Well, first of all, because He is God. Secondly, the promise rises out of the paradoxes of the Kingdom. The things we cling to wind up slipping through our fingers. On the other hand, "letting go" is actually an expression of trust in the Lord.

> He who loves his life will lose it, and he who hates his life in this world will keep it for eternal life.[226]

Some of the paradoxes of the Kingdom are beautifully expressed in the Prayer of St. Francis.

---

[224] Luke 11:9-13
[225] Matthew 6:33
[226] John 12:25

Oh Divine Master, grant that I may not
so much seek to be consoled as to console;
to be understood as to understand;
to be loved as to love;
for it is in giving that we receive;
it is in pardoning that we are pardoned;
and it is in dying that we are born to Eternal Life."[227]

It is in living in the Kingdom and investing in its precepts that we experience its riches. The principle of reciprocity (see "Sowing and Reaping") demonstrates this powerfully. We get forgiveness by offering it. We receive by giving. We rise by dying. Jesus calls the weary to be yoked with Him and get to work in order to find rest.

Come to Me, all *you* who labor and are heavy laden, and I will give you rest. 29 Take My yoke upon you and learn from Me, for I am gentle and lowly in heart, and you will find rest for your souls. 30 For My yoke *is* easy and My burden is light."[228]

The result of being yoked is rest. To become a bondservant of Christ is to know perfect freedom. To lay down one's life is to discover love's true reward. At first, it sounds backwards, like the Kingdom demands that we give things up, but exactly the opposite is true. The claim of the world and the flesh is that indulgence will yield satisfaction, but it's a lie. The more we acquire, the more our appetite to consume increases, but the less fulfillment we actually experience. The more we rationalize and indulge sin, the easier it

---

[227] While attributed to St. Francis, this prayer doesn't actually appear in print until 1912. It may have been written by a French priest called Father Bouquerel, and was published in *La Clochette*, n° 12, déc. 1912, p. 285
[228] Matthew 11:28-30

becomes, but the more destructive. Rather than giving us life, its legacy is death, but it comes so magnificently packaged most of us swill it down until our conscience dims and our hearts grow hard.

Chapter Eighteen

Three Prizes
The Banquet
The Groom
The City

Though we are confident in what has come to us through the victory of Christ and His willingness to share it with us, there is a dimension of expectation longing for the time when we will no longer bear the weight of sin at all.

> Brethren, I do not count myself to have apprehended; but one thing *I do,* forgetting those things which are behind and reaching forward to those things which are ahead, __14__ I press toward the goal for the prize of the upward call of God in Christ Jesus.[229]

Passages like this remind us that there is a prize, but they also present something of a challenge. We live with the tension of a new life in Christ that is victorious, yet we still live in a fallen world. Jesus addressed the situation by treating us as righteous people even though we are not yet completely acting like it.

> "You are the light of the world. A city that is set on a hill cannot be hidden. __15__ Nor do they light a lamp and put it under a basket, but on a lampstand, and it gives light to all *who are* in the house. __16__ Let your light so shine before men, that they may see your good works and glorify your Father in heaven.[230]

---

[229] Philippians 3:13-14
[230] Matthew 5:14-16

Theologians describe the tension with two terms. *Justification* is being called (and treated) as though we are sinless and righteous. *Sanctification* is when we actually come to the place where we are sinless and righteous.

There is a powerful difference in the way things "worked" in the Old Testament and in the Kingdom. In the first covenant, when something unclean came into contact with something, the "uncleanness" was transmitted. In other words, if a person touched something that was unclean, they then became defiled, even if they were unaware.

> "Or if a person touches any unclean thing, whether *it is* the carcass of an unclean beast, or the carcass of unclean livestock, or the carcass of unclean creeping things, and *[even if]* he is unaware of it, he also shall be unclean and guilty.[231]

In the new covenant, the Kingdom works differently. Holiness can be transmitted. When Jesus touches something unclean, He makes it holy!

> Now a leper came to Him, imploring Him, kneeling down to Him and saying to Him, "If You are willing, You can make me clean."
> 41 Then Jesus, moved with compassion, stretched out *His* hand and touched him, and said to him, "I am willing; be cleansed."[232]

The same thing is supposed to happen with us. We are supposed to go throughout the earth as ambassadors of the Kingdom, touching brokenness and things unclean, calling them to life and holiness.

---

[231] Leviticus 5:2
[232] Mark 1:40-41

When Jesus commissioned us He said, "As the Father has sent me, so also I send you."[233] That means the ministry of the gathered body of Christ should be absolutely indistinguishable from that of Jesus Himself. We are supposed to touch the unclean and make it holy. We are supposed to love the unlovely. We are supposed to lay down our lives and even share redemption.

> And a certain man lame from his mother's womb was carried, whom they laid daily at the gate of the temple which is called Beautiful, to ask alms from those who entered the temple; 3 who, seeing Peter and John about to go into the temple, asked for alms. 4 And fixing his eyes on him, with John, Peter said, "Look at us." 5 So he gave them his attention, expecting to receive something from them. 6 Then Peter said, "Silver and gold I do not have, but what I do have I give you: In the name of Jesus Christ of Nazareth, rise up and walk." 7 And he took him by the right hand and lifted *him* up, and immediately his feet and ankle bones received strength. 8 So he, leaping up, stood and walked and entered the temple with them—walking, leaping, and praising God.[234]

God has accomplished what He set out to do. On the Cross, Jesus cried out, "It is finished."[235] He had done everything that was necessary for Him to do to accomplish our salvation and sanctification.

There are many passages that point to the finished work and encourage us with our new place in Christ. For example, in the opening passage of Ephesians, Paul lists a host of things that we

---

[233] John 20:21
[234] Acts 3:3-8
[235] John 19:30

have in Christ. He does not just speak of what we *will* have, but what we *already have.*

> In Him we have redemption through His blood, the forgiveness of sins, according to the riches of His grace 8 which He made to abound toward us in all wisdom and prudence, 9 having made known to us the mystery of His will, according to His good pleasure which He purposed in Himself, 10 that in the dispensation of the fullness of the times He might gather together in one all things in Christ, both which are in heaven and which are on earth—in Him. 11 In Him also we have obtained an inheritance, being predestined according to the purpose of Him who works all things according to the counsel of His will, 12 that we who first trusted in Christ should be to the praise of His glory. 13 In Him you also *trusted,* after you heard the word of truth, the gospel of your salvation; in whom also, having believed, you were sealed with the Holy Spirit of promise, 14 who is the guarantee of our inheritance until the redemption of the purchased possession, to the praise of His glory.[236]

Look at the abundance of what we have:
- redemption through his blood
- the forgiveness of sins
- the mystery of His will
- an inheritance
- [the ability to live] to the praise of His glory
- the promise of being sealed with the Holy Spirit

And yet, there are times when we (...ok, "I") fall miserably short of the promise. It is some consolation to be in good company, however.

------

[236] Ephesians 1:7-14

For what I am doing, I do not understand. For what I will to do, that I do not practice; but what I hate, that I do. 16 If, then, I do what I will not to do, I agree with the law that *it is* good. 17 But now, *it is* no longer I who do it, but sin that dwells in me. 18 For I know that in me (that is, in my flesh) nothing good dwells; for to will is present with me, but *how* to perform what is good I do not find. 19 For the good that I will *to do,* I do not do; but the evil I will not *to do,* that I practice. 20 Now if I do what I will not *to do,* it is no longer I who do it, but sin that dwells in me.[237]

Here is Paul who was chosen by God to pen (under the inspiration of the Holy Spirit of course) the bulk of the New Testament, painfully sharing his struggle to be faithful and the frustrations of failure.

Recently, I heard a preacher speak on this passage. He said, "*Obviously,* Paul was speaking about his life *before* encountering Christ."

A few days later, a well-seasoned pastor I know named Dudley Hall asked me how the session had gone with the speaker I had heard. I told him, "Well, he said that in Romans 7 Paul was talking about *before* he met Christ. When we are in Christ, he says that we have total victory and complete triumph in every conflict."

Dudley replied, "Yeah," then paused, and said, "Wouldn't it be great if that were true."

Here's the problem. Jesus really was *victorious* on the Cross, and He has made it clear that he wants to share the fullness of that victory

---

[237] Romans 7:15-20

with us. He wants to do much more than we have allowed Him to do in our lives, but we still fall short. Sometimes we crash.

So, what are we to do? We have to cling tenaciously to Scripture's promise that God is good. He is always good. He only does good, and He loves us. We need to keep pressing in to God and keep asking him to work in and around our lives. When something happens that we don't understand (or something *doesn't* happen) we just have to trust Him. With all the references of Jesus calling us to extend the Kingdom, it just doesn't make any sense that He didn't really mean it. If we will seek, yearn, and ask, we *will* see more Kingdom fireworks. Try it for yourself. I have seen more wonderfully miraculous things in the last several years than I had seen in the previous thirty. What's the difference? When priorities are right and the Kingdom of God is sought as the first priority, Kingdom fruit follows.

It is true that there will be a "new heaven and a new earth" when God will manifest His Kingdom fully and totally forever. In the meantime, there is certainly more.[238]

The Banquet
In the opening verses of Genesis, as God is creating, He looks at what He is doing and says, "It is good." Actually, He speaks Hebrew and says, "Tov!" (טוב which means *good*). Over and over as He creates, He sees that it is good. In Hebrew, there is no way of saying something is good, better, or best. For example, to say something is ultimately holy, you would say "holy, holy, holy." When God repeats over and over that creation is good, He is saying good, good, good. "Tov," He says (essentially), "Tov, tov, maseltov!" the epitome of a party. Bishop Bill Frey, who has served as a pastor, a missionary bishop, and a seminary dean, often says it

---

[238] Revelation 22:1

is crucial to remember that God is a party kind of a guy. He loves to laugh and celebrate.

Jesus, too (despite His undeserved somber reputation among some), was fond of a party as well. His first miracle was at a party. His promise for His people is that we will be called to a heavenly banquet, the marriage supper of the Lamb.[239] It is prefigured when we share in the Lord's Supper, but it will be fulfilled in heaven.

The Groom
Images abound in Revelation as John is writing about what God showed him, and he tried to put it into understandable language to share with others. Some people think he was writing in code to get it past the Romans, but I think it is more likely that he was having a hard time finding the words to describe the fantastic things he saw. Writing about the church, he penned:

> 1 Now I saw a new heaven and a new earth, for the first heaven and the first earth had passed away. Also there was no more sea. 2 Then I, John, saw the holy city, New Jerusalem, coming down out of heaven from God, prepared as a bride adorned for her husband. 3 And I heard a loud voice from heaven saying, "Behold, the tabernacle of God *is* with men, and He will dwell with them, and they shall be His people. God Himself will be with them *and be* their God. 4 And God will wipe away every tear from their eyes; there shall be no more death, nor sorrow, nor crying. There shall be no more pain, for the former things have passed away."[240]

---

[239] Revelation 19:9
[240] Revelation 21:1-4

When Jesus died, the veil of the temple was rent in two. It was the curtain that separated people from the holy of holies. After Jesus shed His blood, He forever opened access for us into the holiest place, the very presence of God. But we are not left to just be bystanders. We are invited to share a relationship so sweet, it can only be described in the intimacy of marriage. In this marriage, Jesus is the bridegroom and we—the Church—are His bride. He not only loves us, but He is working in us until we become a bride "without spot or wrinkle."[241] That means that He has a lot of work to do if we are to actually become holy. Eventually, we will come to *know* Him with all the special intimacy (and more) that is found in the best moments of the finest marriages. Keep in mind that God is not overlooking the physical joys that come with marriage. He is no prude. He uses language that we can understand if we have ears to hear. Our relationship with the bridegroom will continue to get more and more amazing.

The City

When we seek the Kingdom, we move toward our inheritance, whether *we* see progress or not. One of the great promises is that *we will come* into the New Jerusalem. The New Jerusalem is an image of the Body of Christ in heaven that Jesus described as a city "set on a hill." Besides the literal fulfillment of Jerusalem being up in the heights, the New Jerusalem is a city that is filled with the people, presence, and light of God, as the whole Church that has come into perfect unity with God and with each other. We must work towards unity today, for it is the substance of our future. Leslie Newbingin wrote, "the Church is not to be defined by what it is, but by the End to which it moves."[242] In breathtaking imagery, its streets are gold, its atmosphere luminous, and its relationships are

---

[241] Ephesians 5:27
[242] Lesslie Newbigin, *The Household of God.* (New York: Friendship Press, 1954.) Page 19.

magnificent. In what is more like a dance than a diagram, the building materials are described as gemstones and sometimes, so are we. Whatever lack of clarity there may be in the imagery, it is impossible to miss the overriding message that God wants us to know it is a place that is wonderful beyond imagination.

> Now the wall of the city had twelve foundations, and on them were the names of the twelve apostles of the Lamb. 15 And he who talked with me had a gold reed to measure the city, its gates, and its wall. 16 The city is laid out as a square; its length is as great as its breadth. And he measured the city with the reed: twelve thousand furlongs.[243] Its length, breadth, and height are equal...21 The twelve gates *were* twelve pearls: each individual gate was of one pearl. And the street of the city *was* pure gold, like transparent glass. 22 But I saw no temple in it, for the Lord God Almighty and the Lamb are its temple. 23 The city had no need of the sun or of the moon to shine in it, for the glory of God illuminated it. The Lamb *is* its light.[244]

Prophetic Promises and Current Struggles
When we fix our eyes on the New Jerusalem as one of the first images of the heavenly prize, it gives us pictures and reminders of *who* we really are and *how* we are to live. It is difficult to know exactly how the images are meant to be understood, but there are some things we can say that help to illuminate our understanding of the Kingdom.

Given how poorly people of faith were able to work out the precise meanings of the various Old Testament prophecies about Jesus, it is

---

[243] I'm not sure of the significance, but I find it interesting that twelve thousand furlongs equals *exactly* 1500 miles.
[244] Revelation 21:14-23

a bit risky to speak authoritatively about the eschatological ones. In the Old Testament, people looked for a coming king, a suffering servant, and a Son of God all as different individuals. It was only in retrospect that we see them all fulfilled in Jesus.

As we look at the prophecies of the New Jerusalem, there are many helpful observations that can be made without having to say that any particular image represents a specific meaning.

It is possible, however, to make some observations about the City we will inhabit for eternity. In fact, the City of God is synonymous with the Kingdom of God. When the Kingdom is fully and finally come, we will be in the midst of the New Jerusalem and we will dwell in it forever.

The heart of the City is very different from the heart of the fallen world. In his work, "On the City of God," Augustine wrote:

> Of the Nature of the Two Cities, the Earthly and the Heavenly.
>
> Accordingly, two cities have been formed by two loves: the earthly by the love of self, even to the contempt of God; the heavenly by the love of God, even to the contempt of self. The former, in a word, glories in itself, the latter in the Lord. For the one seeks glory from men; but the greatest glory of the other is God, the witness of conscience. The one lifts up its head in its own glory; the other says to its God,
>
> "Thou art my glory, and the lifter up of mine head."[245] [246]

---

[245] Schaff, *op. cit.*, P 283.

274

Currently, we live in the Kingdom of God and envision "The City." Eventually, we will see it in fullness and, as with so many other things of God, will "know as we have been known."[247]

To get an idea of what The City is like *"all"* we have to do is imagine the world in which we live, but without sin. No disease, no tears, no pain. No failure, no disappointment, no lack. No wounds, no bondage, no fear. Surely there will still be symphonies of praise to compose, books of testimonies to God's greatness to write, clay and gold to sculpt to honor Him, and whirling dances of delight to offer to Him Who sits on the throne.

At the same time, we need to raise our expectations to live up to what (and who) Jesus says we are.

---

[246] Psalm 3:3
[247] 1 Corinthians 13:12

275

Conclusions

How Then Shall We Live...

This is where we are today. The Lord of the Church, the King of the Kingdom is here. He wants to do more than we can hope or imagine. He has revealed the patterns, laws, principles, and pillars of the Kingdom.[248]

Remember the words of Isaiah that Jesus quoted at the start of His ministry:

> The Spirit of the Lord GOD *is* upon Me,
>> Because the LORD has anointed Me
>> To preach good tidings to the poor;
>> He has sent Me to heal the brokenhearted,
>> To proclaim liberty to the captives,
>> And the opening of the prison to *those who are* bound;
>
> 2   To proclaim the acceptable year of the LORD,
>> And the day of vengeance of our God;
>> To comfort all who mourn,
>
> 3   To console those who mourn in Zion,
>> To give them beauty for ashes,
>> The oil of joy for mourning,
>> The garment of praise for the spirit of heaviness;
>> That they may be called trees of righteousness,
>> The planting of the LORD, that He may be glorified."[249]

To those who live in a fallen, sinful world, this is amazing news. It really is beyond what we could dare to ask—so magnificent that it

---

[248] Matthew 13:11
[249] Isaiah 61:1-3

really couldn't rise from our imagination unless He calls it to life. But the miracle doesn't stop there. Jesus calls us not just to experience the wonders of the Kingdom for ourselves, but to join in its work and its glories. After He has loved us, healed us, and set us free from all manner of life's bondages, as he opens our eyes and heals our broken hearts, He commissions and challenges us to join in extending the Kingdom.

> And they shall rebuild the old ruins,
>> They shall raise up the former desolations,
>> And they shall repair the ruined cities,
>> The desolations of many generations.[250]

To begin with, we are the object of His ministry and transformation. Once reached, however, we become the *they* who will rebuild the walls for others and raise up the former desolations.

In the C. S. Lewis classic book, the Kingdom of Narnia is frozen and covered with ice in the deathly grip of the evil Queen. When Aslan the lion, acting as the Christ-figure, walks through Narnia, however, spring breaks out wherever He steps.

> *Wrong will be right when Aslan comes in sight,*
> *At the sound of his roar, sorrows will be no more,*
> *When he bares his teeth, winter meets its death*
> *And when he shakes his mane, we shall have spring again.[251]*

We ought to live like that. In this cold and fallen world, filled with pain, brokenness, bondage, sickness and disease, Jesus invites us to

---

[250] Isaiah 61:4
[251] C. S. Lewis, *The Lion, the Witch, and the Wardrobe, The Chronicles of Narnia.* (London: Harper Collins 1994). Page 28.

be His agents and live in such a way that the Kingdom of God breaks out wherever we step.

There is no question that the desolated generations wait for deliverance. For most, the wound is so deep that they have little hope that things can ever change, but we are here to convince them. As the Kingdom rises in us and around us, we are forever different. Those who have known the kiss of the Prince, seen Him work, and watched Him transform, find a new hope and a fresh confidence rising within. He can rekindle hope. Even more than that, He can actually restore that which sin and Satan have whittled away.

> Be glad then, you children of Zion,
>> And rejoice in the LORD your God;
>> For He has given you the former rain faithfully,
>> And He will cause the rain to come down for you—
>> The former rain,
>> And the latter rain in the first *month*.
> 24 The threshing floors shall be full of wheat,
>> And the vats shall overflow with new wine and oil.
> 25 "So I will restore to you the years that the swarming locust has eaten,
>> The crawling locust,
>> The consuming locust,
>> And the chewing locust,
>> My great army which I sent among you.
> 26 You shall eat in plenty and be satisfied,
>> And praise the name of the LORD your God,
>> Who has dealt wondrously with you;
>> And My people shall never be put to shame.[252]

---

[252] Joel 2:23-26

No one but God can make that kind of promise. Only He can restore what the evil one had already taken away. The restoration is so magnificent it doesn't just get better from here on. He can actually go back into our hearts and into our past to heal and transform the wounds and the scars that were in our lives. It is the hope of heaven, but it can begin today.

I hadn't seen Tim's mother for almost ten years. It had been a decade since I had held him and rocked him and prayed with him to surrender to Jesus. She had moved and settled into another parish. I was there preaching at the funeral of a dear friend, a bishop who had lost a bout with cancer. After the service she came up to me, tiny and gracefully older, resplendent in one of those purple dresses that suit a matron. She held out both her hands to me, and I looked past the wide-brimmed purple hat into her bright eyes brimming with tears. As she squeezed my two hands tightly, she said intensely, "I have prayed for you and your family absolutely every single day for the last twenty years."

I had always looked back at my time with Tim, when he was dying, and felt that I had fallen short. But she obviously didn't agree. Sometimes more "stuff" of the Kingdom gets done than we know. It is a gift of great substance when we get to learn of some of the fruit we have not known.

"Let's build a city"
Sitting in the outdoor café of the Lilongwe Hotel in Malawi, I was meeting with the Principle Secretary from the Government Ministry of Land. Over early morning coffee I was sharing the vision of working for Community Transformation by starting Christian businesses as launching points for mission. As he listened, he got more and more excited. Eventually, he said, "That sounds exactly like our president's vision. In fact, we have already identified a section of land where we are going to build a city that

is just like what you are describing. Perhaps we could partner together."

Sensing God's blessing and presence (but not having any idea what it would mean!) I reached across the table and shook his hand saying, "Alright then, let's build a city!" (We'll have to see how that develops!)

The challenge, like the Möbius Strip, is to see the ways in which we *already have* what we *will* have. How we can release what God wants us to have in order to share it. God is now giving us in principle what He will give to us in fullness. He doesn't have to, but He chooses to call us to the inspirational and magnificent work of extending the dominion of His Kingdom. Now it's time for us to do what we have been called to do. The Kingdom of God is not just the *Coming* Kingdom, it is also *Here*.